CONGRESS' SECRET $1.17 TRILLION GIVEAWAY

D0104670

CONGRESS' SECRET $1.17 TRILLION GIVEAWAY

#1 BEST-SELLING AUTHOR

ZACH SCHEIDT

Copyright © Agora Financial, LLC, 2018
All rights reserved.

ISBN: 978-1-6212919-2-3

22 21 20 19 18   1 2 3 4 5 6 7

Published by Agora Financial, 808 St. Paul Street, Baltimore, Maryland
www.agorafinancial.com

Cover and Layout Design: Andre Cawley

ACKNOWLEDGMENTS

Pulling this book together so quickly was a team effort. Here are just a few of the people I should thank: Rick Singer-Barnard for compiling my research; Ali Glenn for helping keep me on schedule; Andre Cawley for his design expertise; Erik Kestler, Marina Mamangakis and Chloe Mathers for their fast-paced copyediting; Matt Insley for his leadership; and, of course, my wife and children for inspiring me.

CONTENTS

INTRODUCTION

Compared with many of President Donald Trump's other tweets, this one was pretty tame:

Donald J. Trump ✓
@realDonaldTrump

Follow ⌄

Today, it was my great honor to sign the largest TAX CUTS and reform in the history of our country. Full remarks: 45.wh.gov/TaxCuts

1.84M views · 0:02 / 7:52

President Trump Signs H.R. 1, Tax Cuts & Jobs Bill Act and H.R. 1370
Full Remarks Video: 45.wh.gov/TaxCuts & Transcript: 45.wh.gov/USAHistory

12:47 PM - 22 Dec 2017

Source: Twitter

Trump posted it on Dec. 22, 2017, shortly after signing the Tax Cuts and Jobs Act of 2017 into law.

It was arguably Trump's biggest legislative victory of his first year in office. And while the law is far from perfect—as even some Republicans who voted for it have said—there's no denying it will have a profound effect on the American economy.

In fact, many Americans are already seeing bigger paychecks because of the law. And businesses are announcing they'll see much bigger profits thanks to their lower tax rates. They're also taking advantage of a chance to bring home large chunks of cash they've been forced to keep overseas until now.

Before the Tax Cuts and Jobs Act of 2017, companies only had to pay taxes on profits they brought into the United States. The easy solution, then, was to keep that money in other countries.

With the new law, however, that money is no longer safe from U.S. taxes. More importantly, if they bring it home now, they'll enjoy a very low tax rate. So companies are moving quickly to repatriate their cash.

A large chunk of that cash will be used to reward shareholders with higher dividends and share buybacks—which is no surprise if you read my newsletter *Lifetime Income Report*.

I started telling people how to cash in on Donald Trump's presidency shortly after his tax plan started coming together.

"When Trump lowers the tax rate on overseas cash," I wrote, "a huge chunk of that money will go *straight into the bank accounts of . . . shareholders.*"

I called these impending payouts "Cash for Patriots" checks. All you had to do to receive them was invest in U.S. companies with large overseas cash reserves they'd feel compelled to bring home.

One of the businesses I highlighted was tech giant Apple (AAPL). Sure enough, after the tax plan was ratified, the company announced it was bringing $285 billion back to American shores. It has since announced plans to increase its annual dividend payouts.

Of course, the cash repatriation part of the law wasn't exactly a secret—Trump first floated the idea when he was running for president back in September 2015. (Most of the mainstream media still considered him a joke candidate, so they ignored his policy positions like this.)

But looking at the obvious benefits for investors got me wondering if there were other ways to cash in on the Tax Cuts and Jobs Act of 2017.

Such a sweeping piece of legislation was bound to offer some quiet kick-backs for the politicians who voted for it. So I started digging into the law's nuts and bolts, looking for provisions that weren't getting much attention

Sure enough, there was a last-minute add-on to the bill that would enrich many of the congressmen and senators who supported the legislation. They set themselves up to receive large, regular checks with a greatly reduced tax burden. By my count, these payouts could total up to $1.17 trillion—possibly more!

That's a lot of money . . . and even the greediest folks in Washington knew that voters would notice payouts this big. So to make it "fair," they set it up so they'll collect these checks in a roundabout, low-key—and 100% legal—way. Since everyday investors can follow the same strategy, the politicians can claim they've done nothing wrong.

Of course, the only way to collect a portion of these $1.17 trillion "Congressional Checks" for yourself is to know the strategy. That's why I've rushed this book into production: to quickly bring you up to speed.

I'll tell you everything you need to know about these tax-advantaged "Congressional Checks" and the specific steps you can take to receive them—enjoying the exact same tax benefits the politicians wrote for themselves into law.

But time is of the essence, so let's get started!

CHAPTER 1:

SECTION 199A—THE PROVISION THAT COULD PAY YOU THOUSANDS OF DOLLARS EVERY MONTH

When I started digging into the Tax Cuts and Jobs Act of 2017, I quickly worried that I was in over my head. The entire law and its various additions and changes to existing rules top 500 pages . . . each filled with the incomprehensible "legalese" you'd expect from complex legislation.

Of course, that's just what the politicians want. Keeping things complicated is how they get away with cashing in on the laws they pass.

This time, however, they made a critical mistake—accidentally tipping their hand. This is the section of the law that literally made me laugh out loud:

> **PART II—DEDUCTION FOR QUALIFIED BUSINESS INCOME OF PASS-THRU ENTITIES**
> SEC. 11011. DEDUCTION FOR QUALIFIED BUSINESS INCOME.
>
> (a) In General.—Part VI of subchapter B of chapter 1 is amended by adding at the end the following new section:
>
> "SEC. 199A. QUALIFIED BUSINESS INCOME.

Source: U.S. Congress

To the untrained eye, it might look like just more obscure jargon. But as a former hedge fund manager, I knew exactly what this section of the law was talking about. And I had a pretty good feeling that it was added to benefit politicians.

Some quick research proved it.

Part II of the law adds new sections to the tax code that offer incredible tax advantages to certain investments—investments that many of Washington's power players use to earn "bonus" income checks year after year.

According to my research, Darrell Issa, a congressman from California, already reaps at least $410,000 a year from these types of investments. That's more than twice what he makes just for showing up to work each day. And thanks to the last-minute addition to the tax law he voted for, he'll get to keep even more of that money.

He's not the only one, either. Sen. Ron Johnson of Wisconsin makes over $1 million a year thanks to the checks he receives from this class of investments. Sen. Steve Daines of Montana collects a minimum of $485,000, and as much as $4.2 million, a year from this investment. But even that doesn't compare to Bob Corker's take. The senator from Tennessee collects at much as $7 million from these investments.

And thanks to their last-minute addition to the tax law, they'll pay much less taxes on these regular checks' income. It's almost like a special bonus for Congress.

So where are these "Congressional Checks" coming from? The answer is spelled out in the section of the Tax Cuts and Jobs Act of 2017 I showed you earlier . . .

TWO WAYS CONGRESS PAYS ITSELF WITH THE NEW TAX LAW

Part II of the Tax Cuts and Jobs Act of 2017 added a new section to the U.S. tax code—Section 199A. It changed the way income from certain businesses, commonly called "pass-through entities," is taxed.

Pass-through entities are companies that are specifically structured to avoid having to pay corporate income taxes. They do that by "passing through" their tax burden to their shareholders. Essentially, they pay out almost all of their profits to investors, who then have to claim that money as personal income. While that might sound like a bad deal for investors, there are certain deductions and exclusions that make them worthwhile.

There are two broad categories of pass-through entities: real estate investment trusts (REITs) and fiscally transparent entities (FTEs). Both trade on U.S. stock exchanges, meaning you can buy and sell shares just like you would a stock.

REITs were created in the 1960s as a way to help investors pool their money and collectively buy income-producing properties. They encourage people to build and maintain vital structures by spreading the risk among a wide pool of investors while giving them a chance to earn a share of the profits.

Each share of a REIT represents an ownership stake in a real estate venture—anything from a single office building to a group of single-family homes or even hospital buildings. REITs earn money by developing and selling those properties or by renting them out. By investing in a REIT, you are investing in the property it owns without having to do any physical labor or pay for any maintenance.

You then get a share of any profits the REIT collects. By law, REITs must pay at least 90% of their taxable income to shareholders as dividends—cash payments made to shareholders on a regular basis (usually quarterly). That gives REITs some of the highest income yields on Wall Street. In fact, the average REIT yields nearly 4%—twice the average yield of the S&P 500.

The money is paid on a per share basis. So the more shares of the REIT you own, the more cash you'll receive. For example, if the REIT pays 10 cents a share and you own 100 shares, you'll get $10 with each payout. Own 1,000 shares and you'll get $100.

The IRS considers the money you receive "dividend income," which your broker will report on Form 1099-DIV. Thanks to the changes to the tax code, you'll likely owe less taxes on the income in 2017.

Technically, REITs aren't pass-through entities, because they only pass through their tax burden. FTEs, on the other hand, pass through much more.

PASSING TAX SAVINGS ON TO YOU

FTEs took off largely thanks to the Tax Reform Act of 1986 that Ronald Reagan signed into law. Like REITs, they encourage investors to pool their money to create capital-intensive businesses. While that can include real estate, it can also include businesses devoted to making money from things like interest payments and dividends and transporting natural resources.

You can break FTEs into smaller categories, including general partnerships, limited partnerships, master limited partnerships, publicly traded partnerships, limited liability companies and more. The technical structure of each of them is a bit different, but FTEs still operate pretty much the same way—paying nearly all of their profits to investors.

You buy and sell FTEs just like you would a stock. But technically speaking, when you buy an FTE, you're buying "units." (I still call them "shares," just for the sake of convenience.) Each unit represents an investment of capital into the business, which entitles you to part of the profits.

And while that share of the profits is paid to you like a dividend, it's considered a "return of capital." In other words, a return of the money you put into the business.

This is an important distinction when tax time rolls around. Remember, an FTE doesn't pay corporate income taxes. It shifts that burden to unitholders by paying out almost all of the income it makes. But it also passes through certain tax deductions to its unitholders.

As you probably know, businesses get tax deductions for depreciation of their assets—essentially reducing the taxes they owe due to wear and tear on the equipment they use to do their jobs. For instance, a company that relies on heavy construction equipment can lower its reported income simply by accounting for the fact that their machines are worth less now than when they were brand-new.

FTEs own depreciating assets, too. But just as the tax burden is passed through to the FTE's unitholders, so is the depreciation credit. In other words, you can deduct your share of the FTE's depreciation from your return of capital—effectively lowering the amount of taxes you'll owe on that income.

Any other tax credits will be passed through, too. If the deductions exceed the return of capital you received, you won't owe any taxes on the income you've received at all.

If that sounds like a lot to keep track of, don't worry too much. Instead of a 1099-DIV form, your broker or the FTE will send you a Schedule K-1. It will break down how much money you received and how much you can deduct from that total when filing your taxes.

Getting return of capital from an FTE instead of dividends also affects the profits you report when you sell the stock. When you sell a stock for a profit, you have to pay capital gains taxes. It's usually calculated by subtracting what you paid for a stock from the income you made selling it. It's known as the cost basis.

But return of capital reduces your cost basis. Let's say you buy one share (unit) of an FTE for $27. During the year, it sends you checks totaling $2. If you then sell your share for $27—the price you paid for it—the IRS will actually say you profited $2 on the sale. As far as it's concerned, the $2 return of capital you received means you only paid $25 for the FTE.

Dividends, on the other hand, are considered income, so they typically don't affect your cost basis.

So it's better to hold onto your partnership shares for as long as possible. If you're still holding them when you die, the cost basis is reset to its initial value. That means you can leave your beneficiaries an income-paying asset without owing tax on the shielded income you received.

Steady, tax-advantaged income that becomes an asset you can leave to your family guilt-free! Is it any wonder politicians voted to pay lower taxes on these investments?

A GIFT FROM GREEDY POLITICIANS

Now, I completely understand if you're having trouble wrapping your head around the idea of REITs and FTEs. Frankly, I think Wall Street and Washington collaborated to make them as hard to understand as possible, just to discourage everyday people from getting in on the action.

That's because these companies make as much as $1.3 trillion in a single year . . . and must immediately send most of that money back out to shareholders. Assuming they return 90% of their profits, that's $1.17 trillion ending up in investors' accounts.

Luckily, you don't have to fully understand all the intricacies of REITs or FTEs to collect a share of that windfall. Here are the only things you need to know:

1. REITs and FTEs trade on the major exchanges just like stocks, meaning you can buy in through any U.S. stockbroker (more on that in Chapter 2).
2. Once you own shares, you are entitled to a portion of the REIT's or FTE's profits. They avoid taxes by paying out the bulk of what they earn, which means they send some of the biggest checks on Wall Street.
3. The Tax Cuts and Jobs Act of 2017 changed the way the payouts from REITs and FTEs are taxed, meaning you have a chance to keep even more of the money regularly sent out.

In short, Congress' desire to line their own pockets with extra money has given you the tools to benefit, too.

But you need to be careful. A lot of REITs and FTEs were created to take advantage of the law and not all of them are worth buying. Estimates vary, but there could be anywhere from 165–225 REITs trading on the major exchanges, not to mention a large number of FTEs.

To ensure the best payouts, you need to buy the best REITs and FTEs. So in the next chapter, I'll tell you my methods for doing exactly that.

CHAPTER 2:
HOW TO MAKE SURE YOU GET THE BIGGEST, BEST CONGRESSIONAL CHECKS

Pass-through entities like REITs and FTEs pay out up to $1.17 trillion a year, if not more. And U.S. politicians enjoy a large part of that take.

We know this because senators and congressmen are required to fill out financial disclosure forms listing their assets and sources of income. Digging through these files is pretty eye-opening.

International Business Times reviewed the congressional financial disclosures of 44 House and Senate leaders behind the bill. It found they earned between $2.6 million and $16 million from pass-through investments in 2016. The tax bill now lets them deduct some of that income each year.

By the paper's reckoning, the deductions add up to as much as $3.2 million. That's right—a politician who earns $16 million from pass-through real estate investments can declare that the first $3.2 million doesn't count!

(Also, while a lot of the attention has been on the Republicans who voted for the tax bill, Democrats are undoubtedly benefiting, too.)

But as I've said, they get away with this by claiming anyone can enjoy the same tax breaks. And it's true—you can buy into these investments yourself, collect steady income from them and possibly deduct part of the money from your taxes.

Your first step is to buy shares in the REITs and FTEs that pay this newly tax-advantaged income. But it might seem intimidating if you've never bought as much as a single stock before.

So let's quickly run through the basics.

A CRASH COURSE IN INVESTING

Just about every company in existence—including a REIT or FTE—uses stock shares to represent an ownership stake. It makes it clear who has the most say in a company's future, and it helps divvy up profits or assets.

Many of those companies make their shares available to the public, putting them for sale on stock exchanges. People can then buy the shares, essentially becoming part-owners in the business.

But don't get the wrong idea. Companies issue and sell millions, even billions, of shares of stock. So unless you're incredibly wealthy, you'll never own a significant percentage of the company. Instead, investors generally buy stock shares to benefit from a company's success.

There are two ways this can happen. The first is through stock appreciation. Essentially, as the company's value increases, so does the stock's value. Investors hope to sell their stake in the company for a higher price down the road.

The other way is through dividends—the cash payments some companies send to shareholders. For most companies, these payouts are optional. But investors hope that as a company's profits increase, management will increase the company's dividend payouts.

Of course, as I explained, REITs and FTEs must pay out most of their profits to shareholders, so this is less of a concern. If you own shares of pass-through entities like these, you will get payouts as long as the company makes money.

To buy a publicly traded REIT or FTE, you will need to open an account with a stockbroker. Brokers act as middlemen between stock buyers and sellers. You deposit cash with them, which they hold until you want to buy stock. Then they pair you with someone selling the stock you want, taking the money out of your account and paying it to the seller. The broker then transfers the stock share shares to your account.

When you want to sell the stock, the broker reverses the process. They pair you with someone looking to buy the stock you're selling, collect the money, deposit it into your account and transfer the shares out of your account to the new owner.

The broker also handles dividend distributions. It lets the dividend-paying company know how many stock shares its clients own. The company pays the broker enough money to cover those shareholders, and the broker distributes the cash to shareholders.

Dividends are paid out on a per share basis, meaning you get a dividend payment for every share you own. Most companies pay out dividends every quarter, so you can expect to find more money in your account every three months or so.

Obviously, brokerages perform a service, and they get paid for doing what they do. The most basic way brokers do this is with a commission—a fee charged to execute your trades. The commission price can vary wildly from broker to broker.

Of course, the best broker isn't necessarily the one with the lowest commissions. Higher-priced brokers tend to have more tools and guidance available, which can be very helpful for new investors. Lower-cost brokers tend to have few bells and whistles. In fact, many of them cater to more experienced investors. Do a quick Google search for brokers to find one that seems to meet your needs.

Once you've settled on a broker, opened an account and funded it, you're all set to start trading. Your next task is to decide what you want to invest in.

As I said in the last chapter, there are lots of REITs and FTEs to choose from. They're all required to pay out a large chunk of their income, but to do that, they need to make income in the first place.

If you have millions of dollars lying around, you don't have to be too picky—buy enough shares in just a few of them and collect all the tax-advantaged money you can. If some of your holdings run into trouble and stop paying out, you can just keep relying on the other ones you're holding.

But you're likely starting with a smaller sum of money, so you can't really afford the luxury of investing in the wrong pass-through entities. You also need to deploy your money more strategically to make it work as hard as possible.

To do that, you want to find pass-through entities that offer the best payouts. You want those payouts to increase over time. And you want the value of your shares to increase, too, for when you're ready to sell.

So I developed a system to pinpoint investments that meet all three of those requirements.

MY THREE PILLARS OF INVESTING

This strategy forms the basis of my *Lifetime Income Report*, a monthly newsletter I write and publish. It's based on principles I used when I was managing a million-dollar hedge fund to maximize my wealthy clients' income with the least risk.

I absolutely loved the work I did at the fund. And I had a great boss. His name was Bill, and he delivered profits for our customers year after year for 20 years. Not every year was stellar. But every year was a winning year. Not many investors can say that.

Bill once told me something that has stayed with me to this day. He said, "Zach, our clients don't care if we shoot the lights out. But they absolutely require us to protect the money that they have trusted us with."

That principle never left me . . . even when I left to start a business of my own. I decided to share my income strategies with anyone who needed more money for retirement. But I never lost sight of the fact that my advice would put people's money on the line. My old clients could afford some losses, if we had seen any, but the folks I was dealing with now—people just like you—worked too hard to put their cash in harm's way.

So I developed my Three Pillars of Income Investing—a clear set of guidelines to make sure you buy only the safest, most profitable companies out there. They are:

1. **Capital preservation**: We want stable companies with lots of cash and little debt, meaning they can weather any crisis that may crop up.

2. **Growth**: We want to see a company with growing earnings and revenue.

3. **Yield:** We look for companies that have steadily increased dividends.

The Three Pillars can be used to evaluate any company—even REITs and FTEs. If you find a pass-through entity that lives up to all three pillars, you can be sure you're buying a strong, growing company with sustainable payouts.

In the next several chapters, I'll share the names of several pass-through entities that have passed my Three Pillar screens with flying colors. I'll also give you their stock symbols—sometimes known as tickers. These are three–four-letter codes that stockbrokers use to make buying and selling shares easier.

At the very end of each chapter, I'll give you each company's tax identification number. This is how the IRS identifies a company, similar to how it knows you by your Social Security number. In some cases, your tax preparer may want this information, so be sure to keep in handy when it's time to do your taxes.

If you agree with my analysis of the company and want to start collecting checks from it, log into your brokerage account. Look for a place to enter the company's stock symbol and then click that you want to buy the stock. Enter the number of shares you wish to buy and then select the type of order you want.

If you want to buy the stock at any price, use a market order. If you want to choose the maximum you're willing to pay for the stock, use a limit order. Limit orders can expire at the end of the day, or until you cancel using something known as a good-till-canceled (GTC) order. For the most part, if you're not buying a lot of shares—say, less than 1,000—you should be OK using a market order.

Approve the order and your broker will do the rest. Then the next time the company pays out dividends, the money will go directly into your account. And thanks to Congress, when tax time rolls around, you should be able to deduct some of the cash you've received from your total income—reducing what you owe to the IRS.

Just remember that taxes are still very complicated and everyone's situation is different. So check with a tax adviser to make sure you're eligible for these deductions.

With that out of the way, let's get started!

CHAPTER 3:

EARN REGULAR CHECKS AS THE WORLD GOES GREEN

Brookfield Renewable Partners (BEP) is at the forefront of clean energy production—generating electricity without burning fossil fuels. It's already doing quite well for itself, and I expect it to do even better as nation after nation moves away from burning coal and oil to keep the lights on. Renewable is the future.

Over the next 10 years alone, the amount of money spent globally on new power generation capacity is expected to reach $4.37 trillion. Just under half of that total, about $2 trillion, will be directed toward renewable energy.

When you think of renewable energy, you probably think solar and wind. And Brookfield operates some wind farms and is expanding into getting power from the sun. But over 80% of its money comes from "green" electricity that doesn't rely on favorable weather conditions. I'm talking about hydroelectric power.

Hydroelectric power most commonly involves an electric power plant using a dam on a river to capture water in a reservoir. As water is released from that reservoir, it flows through and spins a turbine that activates a generator to create electricity.

The problem with hydroelectric power is that most of the world's best sites for hydropower have already been tapped. Today, hydropower accounts for roughly 16% of the world's electricity, and it isn't going to grow much (if at all) from there.

So Brookfield Renewable Partners finds itself in an enviable position. It's the single largest public owner of hydroelectric power plants on the planet, with 218 hydroelectric power-generating stations built on 82 different rivers.

Brookfield's impossible-to-replicate renewable portfolio

	River Systems	Facilities	Capacity (MW)	LTA (GWh)	Storage (GWh)
Hydroelectric					
North America	50	170	4,847	17,775	4,879
Colombia	6	6	2,732	14,476	4,703
Brazil	26	42	42	4,647	–
	82	218	218	36,898	8,582
Wind					
North America	–	10	10	2,310	–
Europe	–	21	21	1,220	–
Brazil	–	5	5	588	–
	–	36	36	4,118	–
Other	–	6	6	385	–
Total	**82**	**261**	**261**	**41,401**	**8,582**

Source: Brookfield Renewable Partners

These plants make Brookfield pretty immune to competition. After all, it's not like someone can easily build a new hydroelectric station next door. Over 80% of the company's revenue comes from its hydroelectric operations.

Roughly half of Brookfield's business is located in the United States, where it is focused mainly on power markets in New York, Pennsylvania and New England. Brookfield also owns seven wind farms in California, Arizona and New Hampshire.

The rest of Brookfield's operations are split between Canada (15%), Brazil (15%), Colombia (15%) and Europe (15%).

The company's cash flow is derived from fixed-price, long-term contracts, which make it both predictable and stable. Those contracts have prices linked to inflation to ensure Brookfield's revenues increase as its expenses do—perfect for a dividend-paying business.

Those contracts have Brookfield's cash flows locked in for an average duration of 16 years. The counterparties to those contracts are investment-grade-rated, creditworthy counterparties, including public power authorities, distribution companies and industrial users.

Brookfield's counterparties agree to "take or pay" contracts, which means that Brookfield is getting paid for a known volume even if the counterparty doesn't want it.

In other words, both Brookfield's selling price and its volume of sales are locked in. You aren't going to find a safer revenue stream than that. This means you can have great confidence in Brookfield's future cash-generating and dividend-paying abilities.

Furthermore, its operating projects require very little capital spending each year to sustain their cash-generating abilities. Yes, building them costs a lot upfront, but they then generate big cash flows for decades into the future.

Of course, Brookfield isn't the only company in the renewable energy business, but it is one of the few that offer an incredibly reliable (and growing) cash flow stream. As an FTE, it will share most of that money with its shareholders. The company aims to have a distribution payout ratio of 60–70% of its funds from operations and also grow that distribution at a rate of 5–9%.

In other words, it plans to send up to 70% of its profits to shareholders (keeping the rest for emergencies and to invest in new opportunities) . . . and increase the amount of money it sends to shareholders by up to 9% a year.

Since its inception in December 2011, the company has lived up to its strategic plan, delivering annual dividend growth of 6.2%.

Another reason to have faith in the company's stability and growth is its close relation with its parent company. Brookfield Renewable Partners operates as a subsidiary of Brookfield Asset Management, a huge global asset manager. Brookfield Asset Management manages somewhere north of $250 billion in assets spread across power generation, real estate, infrastructure and private equity.

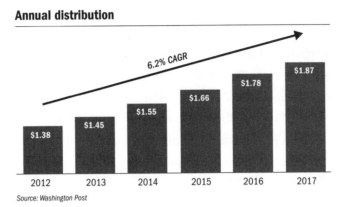

Annual distribution

Source: *Washington Post*

This relationship with Brookfield Asset Management opens up all kinds of world-class opportunities for Brookfield Renewable Partners. The result of that for Brookfield Renewable Partners has been steady, profitable growth through repeated accretive acquisitions.

That is something that I believe we can expect to continue, especially with demand for renewable energy growing.

Brookfield Renewable's current existing project pipeline is ready to add up to $30 million of cash flow by the end of 2019. Note that going forward, wind projects are going to play a bigger role for Brookfield. As I said, there just aren't many hydroelectric investment opportunities.

Brookfield's robust project pipeline

"We have over 300 MW of construction and construction ready-assets expected to contribute $45–50 million of annualized FFO once commissioned."

Project	Region	Technology	Capacity (MW)	Expected commissioning	Expected annualized FFO ($ Million)
Serra dos Caalinhos	Brazil	Hydro	25	25	25
Crockandun	Europe	Wind	15	15	15
Shantavny	Europe	Wind	16	16	16
Silea — Verde 4A	Brazil	Hydro	28	28	28
Slievecallan	Europe	Wind	28	28	28
Ballyhoura	Europe	Wind	19	19	19
Silea — Verda 4	Brazil	Hydro	19	19	19
Tralog	Europe	Wind	19	19	19

Source: *Brookfield Renewable Partners*

Remember, the scarcity of those opportunities is what makes Brookfield's hydroelectric assets so valuable.

Going forward, we can expect to see Brookfield Renewable enter the renewable business in both India and China. The commentary from management is that they see big potential for renewable power development as both of these countries try to meet their growing need for electricity while simultaneously reducing their reliance on coal.

Brookfield Asset Management is already on the ground running in both China and India through other businesses and will undoubtedly be key to opening the door for Brookfield Renewable Partners to seize on opportunities as well.

To put all of that in perspective, let's run Brookfield through my "Three Pillars" checklist.

Capital Preservation: Clean, reliable and renewable energy is the holy grail of the modern world and Brookfield Renewable Partners is one of the leading names in the field. Its hydroelectric power assets alone are scarce and incredibly valuable. They rest on top of a rock-solid balance sheet and locked-in cash flows from long-term fixed take-or-pay pricing contracts.

This is a company that you can sleep well at night owning.

Growth: As I said, the company shoots to grow its distribution over time at an annualized rate of 5–9%. So far, it has more than lived up to its growth targets, having generated an annualized 15% rate of return to shareholders.

Going forward, I think we can expect more of the same as Brookfield steadily adds new renewable projects to its portfolio. There is plenty of opportunity in this sector, especially for a world leader like Brookfield.

Yield: Normally, you wouldn't expect a growing company to pay such a high dividend. But as a leader in the renewable energy business, Brookfield really does have one of the greatest growth opportunities imaginable in front of it. There's no doubt that locking in today's yield is one sweet deal.

In short, Brookfield Renewable Partners offers a unique opportunity to own a piece of some very highly coveted renewable energy assets. Better still, you can get paid a juicy yield for doing so.

The company is structured as a master limited partnership, meaning it's an FTE that passes through its depreciation tax credits to you. That means you may not have to pay taxes on some of the money Brookfield sends you every quarter. You may also benefit from the provisions of the Tax Cuts and Jobs Act of 2017, so you could end up sending even less of your payouts to Uncle Sam.

Action to take: Consider buying Brookfield Renewable Partners (BEP).

Brookfield Renewable Partners trades under the symbol BEP. Its tax identification number is 001-35530.

CHAPTER 4:
COLLECT TEXAS OIL CHECKS

There's a simple reason a lot of the FTEs and REITs on the market aren't worth your time. Yes, they are all required to send most of their profits back to shareholders. But as I touched on earlier, profits are never guaranteed.

So obviously, you want to find companies with the highest profits possible. Not only should they be bringing in a lot of revenue, but they also need to be spending very little on expenses. Everything from employee salaries to loan payments cuts down on the money a company has left to send to shareholders.

That's what I love about this next opportunity. It has little debt and very few employees. It barely spends any money at all. In 2017, it brought in $160 million in revenue, but less than $6.3 million of that went toward general and administrative expenses.

The company is **Viper Energy Partners (VNOM)**. It's a master limited partnership that specializes in collecting oil royalties.

Essentially, Viper owns the mineral rights to land that may have oil under the surface. Rather than drill for the oil itself, it allows other companies to handle the dirty work. In exchange, Viper gets a portion of the revenue from any oil that makes it to market.

In other words, Viper gets paid to let other companies produce oil on its land. Of course, for this scheme to work, Viper needs to have property worth drilling. Not a problem, though, because it owns mineral rights in one of the richest oil deposits on Earth. It's called the Permian Basin, a large swath of land in Texas and part of New Mexico.

The Permian Basin contains an American oil bonanza so large that the only comparable oil play in the world is the mighty Ghawar field in Saudi Arabia.

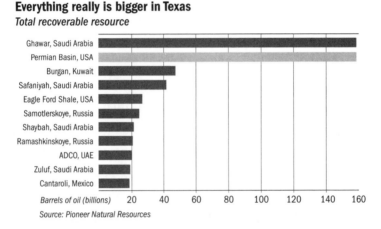

Everything really is bigger in Texas
Total recoverable resource

Source: Pioneer Natural Resources

As you are probably know, oil production in Texas goes way back. The Permian has been churning out oil since the 1920s. In fact, the Permian played a key role in providing the oil that fueled the Allied effort in World War II.

Of course, oil deposits don't last forever—once you pull it out of the ground, it's gone. And by the 1990s, oil companies were having a hard time finding new sources of easy-to-get petroleum in the United States. Unless something changed, it looked like we'd have needed to import most of our crude from then on.

That's what spurred engineers to take another look at shale oil.

Shale is a very porous rock. And we've known for decades that oil is easily trapped inside it. The trick is getting it out. Conventional oil wells essentially pump liquid crude out of the ground, but the oil in a shale deposit doesn't work that way. And while engineers tried to come up with alternative methods, none was considered economically feasible in the long term.

However, with U.S. oil sources running dry and prices on the rise, entrepreneurs decided to have another go at shale oil production. Higher oil prices meant there was a better chance of earning a profit from shale oil, and better technology lowered the productions costs.

The solution turned out to be a combination of horizontal drilling (drilling sideways underground) and multistage fracturing (or fracking, as we know it). It gave American drillers a massive new source of oil.

The first large shale oil play to actually ramp up production was the Bakken in North Dakota. The second was the Eagle Ford in Texas. Then attention finally fell on the Permian Basin, which has by far the most shale oil in place.

America's top shale oil hotspot: the Permian Basin!

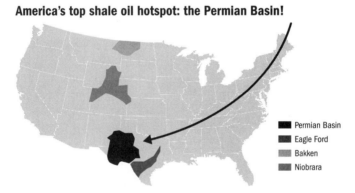

Source: Pioneer Natural Resources

In the Permian, the oil is "stacked" in different zones on top of each other like a layer cake. An absolutely oil-soaked and absurdly valuable layer cake. Because of this layering, one acre of land in the Permian is equivalent to 10 acres of land in another shale play like the Eagle Ford or the Bakken.

So for every dollar a driller spends in the Permian, significantly more oil can be recovered than with a dollar spent in the other shale oil plays. This brings down the price required to make money producing shale oil from the Permian. It also increases how much money a producer can make at every price of oil.

Oil companies are now swarming back into Texas, and Viper has title to land in the very best part of the Permian Basin. Said another way, Viper is the landlord of America's best oil property.

But as I said, Viper doesn't have to lift a finger to do anything with that oil. It simply needs to find a company willing to drill on its land and then it claims a 20% royalty on the oil its partner sells.

By merely owning the mineral rights, Viper doesn't have to pay to drill any wells. It doesn't have to worry about upkeep. I imagine a day in the Viper office consisting of opening the mail and depositing the royalty check in the bank. Nice work if you can get it!

With so few expenses, Viper has an incredibly high-margin business model. In 2017, Viper had $160 million of revenue and generated $138 million of cash flow from operations. The year before, it raked in $79 million of revenue and $68 million of cash flow. In short, most of the revenue Viper receives turns into cash flow.

Most of the company's operating expenses go toward funding new royalty deals—which create new income flows. But since Viper is structured as a master limited partnership, most of the remaining cash must be paid out to shareholders.

The dividend that Viper pays is variable, which means that it fluctuates based on the cash flow that is available to pay a dividend. The key factor is oil prices. Again, Viper gets 20% of the revenue from its partners' oil sales. If prices are low, the revenues will be, too.

But don't let that worry you too much. Viper's high margins still allow it to remain profitable and pay a dividend even at amazingly low oil prices

For example, when oil dipped into the $20s in the first quarter of 2016, Viper still generated free cash flow and still paid a sizable distribution to shareholders. More importantly, it did so without doing any damage to its balance sheet.

So while we can hope for higher oil prices, we can take comfort in the fact that Viper can continue to pay dividends at almost any price.

And don't forget that the company can also tap into new royalty streams. In fact, that's the entire reason Viper was formed in 2014. It's actually a subsidiary of Diamondback Energy, a very well-respected oil and gas producer focused on the Permian Basin.

Diamondback owns approximately 64% of Viper's shares and is therefore in full control of the direction of the business. Diamondback also operates 33% of Viper's royalty acreage. So as Diamondback expands its operations, producing more oil, Viper will receive higher royalty payouts.

In 2017 alone, Diamondback drilled 150 new wells, with 123 going into production. Overall, it increased production by 79%. That's hardly surprising, though, since—as I said—the land it occupies is simply the best oil drilling opportunity in North America today.

Diamondback also has an ambitious growth plan for the next few years, meaning Viper's revenues, cash flows and distributions to shareholders will grow, no matter what oil prices do. In addition, Viper has also bought royalty acres in the Eagle Ford shale deposit in Texas.

So there's a lot to like here. Running it through our Three Pillars sums it all up very nicely.

Capital preservation: Royalty companies are some of the safest opportunities out there, because their only real risk is being unable to find good deals on mineral rights. That's even less of a problem with Viper, because it is tied to Diamondback. And as I've shown, even low oil prices don't put a big dent in its payouts.

Growth: If there is one thing that I feel certain is set to grow over the next 20 years, it is oil production in the Permian Basin. And Viper allows us to get exposure to Permian production growth without having to worry about what the price of oil is going to do. This company has excellent growth prospects.

Yield: Viper's distribution is going to fluctuate quarter to quarter, depending on how much cash flow Viper generates. So yes, if oil prices drop, that distribution could go down. On the other hand, production on Viper's land is virtually certain to increase. The new revenue will almost certainly make up for any shortfalls in the oil price. That means Viper could still increase its quarterly payouts even if oil prices took a dive.

In short, Viper is a uniquely high-cash-flow-margin business with the ownership rights to some very uniquely profitable oil assets. As a master limited partnership, it's required to send out a large portion of that cash flow to its investors. And as with all the examples I'll tell you about in this book, you can expect to pay lower taxes on the money you receive thanks to the Tax Cuts and Jobs Act of 2017.

Action to take: Consider buying shares of Viper Energy Partners (VNOM).

Viper Energy Partners trades under the symbol VNOM. Its tax identification number is 46-5001985.

CHAPTER 5:
EARN MEATY CHECKS FROM A LEGENDARY "VULTURE INVESTOR"

The word "vulture" brings to mind a group of big, ugly birds standing around a dead animal, gleefully picking at the corpse.

So you'd think being called a vulture would be an insult. But not to Howard Marks. He and his company **Oaktree Capital Group LLC (OAK)** have earned a reputation for being "vulture investors"—a label they wear with pride.

Oaktree is a private equity firm. That means it manages money for private entities like pension funds, foundations, insurance companies and more. It essentially takes clients' money and invests it for them.

It may sound like a boring business but the profits it sees are nothing to snore at. It has three ways of making money:

- Charging management fees for investing its clients' massive amounts of money
- Collecting performance fees—a percentage of any profits it makes for its investors
- Investing its own money in ventures alongside their clients' cash.

For investors, Oaktree's business model offers a near-perfect formula. Oaktree's clients pay no matter how their investments perform, guaranteeing Oaktree also has a steady inflow of cash. But Oaktree has a huge incentive to make sure those investments perform well—earning a percentage of the profits it makes for clients. The company also directly benefits from any successful investments made with its own money.

Of course, that means it will only see big profits if it makes smart investments. But that's no concern with Marks helping call the shots.

Marks is listed on *Forbes* as one of America's 400 wealthiest people. He got there by being a vulture investor. That just means he bought cheap assets from troubled companies and then sold them at a profit.

It might sound distasteful, but just like actual vultures, what Marks and Oaktree do is beneficial. They buy investments that no one else will touch, giving people a chance to recoup some of their capital. Then they help the troubled companies turn things around, keeping their doors open and returning them to profitability.

During the last financial crisis in 2008, Marks became famous for buying up bonds of companies that seemed headed for bankruptcy.

Bonds are essentially how companies borrow money from investors. Each bond represents a fixed amount of money owed to the investor, usually $1,000 per bond, plus regular interest payments. But the bond's value is determined by how likely a company is to pay that money back.

Needless to say, when a company is in trouble, its bond prices plummet. Investors don't have any faith the company will repay its debts, much less keep up with its interest payments. So people start selling their bonds.

Many companies found themselves in this situation when the recession hit. Bonds worth $1,000 were selling for $700, $600, even $500 or less—because investors didn't think the company would be around long enough to repay the bond's $1,000 face value.

So Marks was able to buy up corporate bonds cheap. He and his team then used their knowledge and list of contacts to help the companies get back on their feet. Many of them were able to pay their debt obligations to Marks and Oaktree. The moves added as much as $330 million to Marks' wealth alone.

Buying troubled bonds is still a key pillar of Oaktree's strategy, and it's not the only way the company benefits from "vulture" tactics.

Oaktree also buys up stock of good companies that have found themselves on the rocks. Oaktree tries to gain enough of a stake in the business to have a say in its future. It's called "control investing." Again, by helping a company fix its business, Oaktree helps it and its clients make more money.

Then there are Oaktree's investments in the real estate market. It buys up mortgages from businesses and people who are behind on their payments. While that could allow Oaktree to foreclose on the property, that's not its goal. Instead, it does its best to restructure the debt, allowing folks to stay in their homes or business locations under a repayment structure they can live with.

Of course, Oaktree doesn't just give money to troubled businesses and people. It strategically chooses its opportunities to assure the best potential profits for the least amount of risk. For instance, solid companies can get in trouble if they borrow too much money. But if Oaktree sees the business itself is sound, it may decide the company is worth investing in. It will then use its influence to get the company to focus on its core business while reducing its debt.

And while this distressed investing is very lucrative part of Oaktree's investment portfolio, it's far from the only part. In fact, it has a sizeable chunk of its capital in safer, reliable investments to provide gains if some of its riskier bets don't pay off.

As you can see in the pie chart on the next page everyday corporate debt—this is, bonds—make up 43% of Oaktree's holdings. These kind of bonds are the safest you can buy. The company also has 5% of its money in listed equities—the regular stocks you and I can buy.

Investing like this gives Marks and his team more breathing room to invest in riskier assets. At last count, nearly a quarter of their money was in the distressed debt opportunities I've discussed earlier. And 14% of their assets are being used for control investing.

Thanks to Marks' reputation for making money even in the worst market conditions, Oaktree's client list continues to grow. At last count, it was managing money for 75 of the 100 largest U.S. pension funds. It also handles funds for 369 colleges, endowments and foundations. It even manages

16 sovereign wealth funds—essentially the investments of a country's government.

Oaktree's division of assets under management

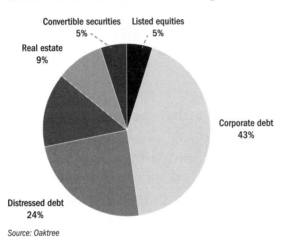

Source: Oaktree

You can find an Oaktree office in 13 counties, nestled in economic hotspots like New York, London, Frankfurt, Hong Kong, Tokyo and Beijing. All told, the company was managing $100 billion worth of assets as

Oaktree's rapid rise in money management
OAK assets under management

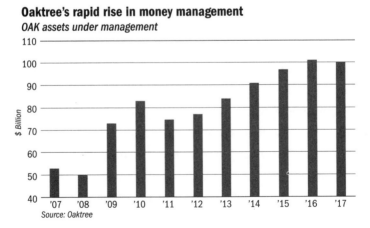

Source: Oaktree

of the end of 2017, up from $53 billion a decade before.

The company also reported excellent profits in 2017, coming in a full $128 million higher than 2016's numbers.

Remember, that money comes from three sources—the fees Oaktree charges its clients, a cut of the profits it delivers to clients plus the profits it makes with its own money. And by investing in OAK, you're literally making yourself a partner in Marks' business. Since Oaktree is a master limited partnership, you'll receive quarterly payments that are tied directly to the management fees and performance fees that Oaktree Capital Group generates.

The downside is that the dividend you receive can vary wildly from one quarter to the next, as the chart below shows:

Oaktree's quarterly distribution depends on OAK's performance

Source: Yahoo Finance

Still, in its worst year so far, 2015, the company paid out a total of $2.10 a share. And as you can see, 2017 was a great year for payouts, with the total for the year topping $3.21. The company pledges to return as much of its capital as it can to shareholders.

Even better, the company will look for opportunities to buy back its shares at good prices. These buyback programs reduce the number of shares available, making the remaining shares on the market more valuable.

Let's quickly see how the company stands up to the Three Pillars.

Capital preservation: Howard Marks designed Oaktree Capital to thrive when markets are at their worst. Clients have come to trust the wisdom of him and his team. And that team is incentivized to get the biggest, safest gains possible. That gives me great confidence in this company.

Growth: If there's a downside to the Oaktree strategy, it's the fact that it works best when investors are running scared. The markets started surging after Donald Trump's election victory, making it harder to find distressed opportunities. But things are starting to look a little wobbly and some very good companies will undoubtedly make some bad decisions. Oaktree is keeping plenty of powder dry in case that happens . . . which could spark tremendous growth.

Yield: Since Oaktree's cash distributions are performance based, your payouts could vary wildly from one quarter to the next. But I trust Marks and his team to continue delivering steady gains for their clients, which will mean steady payouts for us year after year. Remember, the better Oaktree does, the more everyone involved in the company—from its clients to its investors—wins.

The bottom line really is that Oaktree literally lets you partner with one of the world's savviest vulture investors. Jump in now when distressed companies are harder to find so you'll be in place when those juicy, inevitable opportunities arise.

Action to take: Consider buying shares of Oaktree Capital Group (OAK).

Oaktree Capital Group shares trade under the symbol OAK. Its tax identification number is 26-0174894.

CHAPTER 6:

ANOTHER ALL-WEATHER PAYOUT MACHINE TO EXPLORE

Oaktree isn't the only private equity business that made smart moves during the last recession. It's not even your only opportunity to partner up with a great financial mind—earning oversized payouts no matter what the market throws your way.

Allow me to introduce you to the **Blackstone Group LP (BX)**.

Like Oaktree, Blackstone manages the investments of very wealthy clients. It earns its money the same way, too. It earns fees, collects a percentage of the gains it delivers to its clients and profits on the investments it makes with its own money.

One of the biggest differences between Blackstone and Oaktree is size. At last count, Oaktree was managing about $100 billion. As of the end of 2017, Blackstone had $434 billion under management. It is, in fact, one of the largest private equity firms in the world.

The company was founded in 1985 by Peter Peterson and Stephen Schwarzman. Its original goal was to offer other companies advice on mergers and acquisitions. Just two years later, it decided to expand its business opportunities by becoming an investment manager.

Schwarzman is still chairman and CEO of the company. While Marks at Oaktree became famous for buying up bonds during the last financial crisis, Schwarzman gained notoriety by focusing on the real estate market.

Back then, the banks had extended millions of loans to homeowners who couldn't pay them back. When these homeowners defaulted, the banks foreclosed and repossessed the homes. And they didn't know what to do with them. There were no buyers in the collapsing market.

That's when Blackstone stepped up to the plate . . .

It bought more than $8 billion worth of individual homes. And because the banks were so desperate, Blackstone paid only pennies on the dollar for the homes. By 2015, the value of those homes had increased dramatically from the crisis days—and Blackstone started winding down its real estate holdings, collecting and distributing immense profits in the process.

Blackstone also focuses on distressed companies, much like Oaktree. But Blackstone's stance is a little more aggressive. Forget buying bonds or large stakes—Blackstone buys the whole thing outright. Once it owns the entire company, it has the ability to make every decision necessary to improve the profitability of the company.

In some cases, that means firing people or laying them off—which doesn't make Schwarzman many friends in the media. But there's no arguing with the success this has led to.

Consider the case of the Hilton hotel chain. Starting with a single hotel in 1919, Conrad Hilton grew his company to become one of the most recognizable brand names in the world. But by the 2000s, the company's profits were slipping and it was looking at huge bills to renovate and update its properties.

Blackstone saw an opportunity, offering to pay $26 billion for the entire company. It was the largest hotel deal ever at the time. But Blackstone didn't use money it had lying around to make the deal. It borrowed a substantial portion of the cash it needed for the purchase.

So when the 2008 financial crisis struck, it looked like Blackstone had made a very bad move. The company persevered, though, cutting costs, improving revenue and paying down debt. When things were at their worst, the company negotiated with its creditors.

By 2013, the economy had recovered and Blackstone was ready to take Hilton public again. That meant it would allow everyday investors to buy Hilton's stock through what's called an initial public offering. Since Blackstone would be selling the stock, it would receive all the money investors paid for those first shares.

It became the largest initial public offering for a hotel stock ever. And thanks to its smart use of borrowed money, Blackstone's return was double its investment on the deal. Of course, it also held onto a large chunk of Hilton's shares for itself, selling them as needed for the best profits.

It received $2.69 billion by selling some of its stake in 2015, $6.5 billion for part of its share in 2016 and $900 million by selling more shares in 2017. Today, it owns just a 10% stake in Hilton.

Another good example of Blackstone's uncanny ability to get the most for its money is its purchase of SeaWorld in 2009. SeaWorld was part of the Busch Entertainment Corp., a subsidiary of the Anheuser-Busch company. That's Anheuser-Busch, as in the beer company. SeaWorld was part of a package that included Busch Gardens amusement parks.

While the theme parks were performing well in 2009, Anheuser-Busch wanted to focus on its core brewing business and pay down some debt. So Blackstone took the parks off its hands for $2.7 billion. Once again, Blackstone took out loans to pay for the acquisition. It renamed the company SeaWorld Parks & Entertainment.

In 2013, Blackstone took SeaWorld public, earning money from selling shares of the company. But in 2014, SeaWorld saw enormous public backlash from its purported mistreatment of animals in its park, including its signature killer whales. As SeaWorld's ticket sales fell, Blackstone started selling its stake in the company. It completely divested itself in 2017—essentially tripling its money over the seven years or so it owned the company.

That wasn't the only time Blackstone was in the amusement park business. It was also a part-owner of Universal Orlando, home to movie-themed rides and attractions, until 2011. That's when it sold its stake for a cool $1 billion.

The company also won't hesitate to buy into companies that will help improve its mission. In 2018, Blackstone announced that it had bought a 55% stake in Thomson Reuters' financial and risk business.

You probably know Thomson Reuters as a news provider. When it comes to news, it's second only to The Associated Press in terms of name recognition. But the company's biggest strength is its data—providing in-depth numbers that its clients can trust. Its financial and risk division crunches numbers from many different public and private companies to help its clients make informed decisions.

By buying a controlling stake in Thomson, Blackstone gets access to all of its incredibly useful investment information. This should help Blackstone find new deals more easily. It should also help Blackstone better manage its own risk with its widespread portfolio of investments.

At the same time, Thomson gets access to beneficial information Blackstone has accumulated through its private equity investments. So the quality of Thomson's data should get much stronger through this partnership. And as other investment firms pay to access that information, Thomson's profits will increase, which will filter through to Blackstone.

I haven't even touched on Blackstone's other investment interests, from its credit operations to the infrastructure projects it's helped support. It also has a line of exchange-traded funds, pooled investments that are divided into shares and sold on the regular stock markets. Buying shares makes you part-owner of the fund's assets, allowing everyday investors an inexpensive way to buy into complicated investment strategies. (Blackstone gets fees for running these funds.)

Blackstone moves where the money is hottest
Total AUM by segment (billions $)

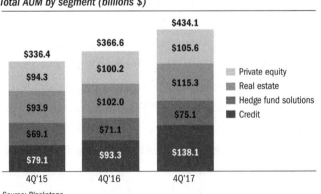

Source: Blackstone

The point is Blackstone has a well-deserved reputation for growing its clients' money. Its assets under management in the fourth quarter of 2017 were up 19% from the year before. For all of 2017, it recorded a 12% increase in the fees it received, a 38% increase in the amount of money it made from investments and a stunning 70% increase in its performance fees!

Like any good company worth your time and attention, it paid out a large sum of that money to shareholders. In 2017, it sent out a record total of $55 billion, good for a payout of $2.32 a share. But like Oaktree, the dividend can vary depending on how the company performs, as the chart below makes clear:

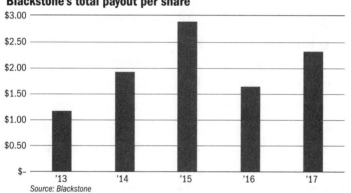

Blackstone's total payout per share

Source: Blackstone

The spike you see in 2015 was directly attributable to Blackstone selling off parts of its real estate portfolio for huge profits. That, of course, decreased the rental revenue it saw in 2016, meaning less of a payout for shareholders.

Still, I'm not too worried about the variable payouts. Blackstone always seems to have a plan, even if it isn't immediately obvious. So I wouldn't be surprised to learn that it's been quietly cultivating another asset that it can unload for immense profits.

Let's put Blackstone through our Three Pillars.

Capital preservation: Blackstone's premise is very similar to Oaktree's, with a proven ability to find great deals in terrible market conditions. There is a little more danger with Blackstone, though, because other people don't always see the wisdom in the company's actions. If the company spends its money without an obvious path to profits, skittish investors could push the share price lower. But as Blackstone has proven again and again, its actions can bear profitable fruit down the road, rewarding anyone who keeps faith.

Growth: You'd think being one of the biggest private equity firms out there would make growth difficult. But Blackstone is always innovating, creating new products for its existing clients and enticing new clients into its ranks. Its assets under management hit a record in 2017, and there's no reason to expect that to slow down anytime soon.

Yield: Yes, the performance-based payouts are a bit of a bummer. But the chances of one or two oversized dividend distributions make it worth the risk, in my opinion. Remember, its per share payout spiked in 2015 as Blackstone cashed in on all the real estate it purchased during the financial downswing. I suspect there are other such opportunities lurking in Blackstone's balance sheet, and I trust its management team to deliver as much money as it can afford to return to shareholders.

In short, while there are plenty of private equity firms out there, I've only found two that meet my Three Pillars criteria. Oaktree and Blackstone take slightly different approaches to the same end—maximizing the money they return to shareholders.

Both are good additions to an income-generating portfolio.

Action to take: Consider buying shares of the Blackstone Group LP (BX).

Blackstone Group trades under the symbol BX. It's tax identification number is 20-8875684.

CHAPTER 7:
MORE CHECKS FROM BLACKSTONE'S SMART STRATEGIES

In the last chapter, I explained how the Blackstone Group took advantage of the real estate downturn to buy properties very inexpensively. In 2015, it began cashing in on those investments, sending its shareholders a big piece of the proceeds.

If you're sorry you missed those oversized payouts, I have good news for you. There's another way to earn regular checks from Blackstone's remaining real estate holdings.

In 2012, Blackstone acquired Capital Trust, a REIT that makes its money with commercial real estate loans. In 2013, it renamed the company **Blackstone Mortgage Trust (BXMT)**.

Blackstone Mortgage Trust makes money in two ways. It can make mortgage loans directly to customers, or it can buy older mortgages that other institutions have made. Its target customers are commercial real estate buyers looking for loans of $50–500 million. As you might expect, that limits the company's pool of potential clients. It's a low-volume, larger-dollar-amount lender, meaning every single loan is put through an extensive due-diligence wringer.

BXMT lent out a total of $4.8 billion in 2017—up from $3.5 billion in 2016—and has a total loan portfolio of $11.1 billion. Most of these loans are made against properties in the United States, with some lending in

Canada and Europe. The map below from BXMT's 2017 year-end report shows where the company has loan exposure:

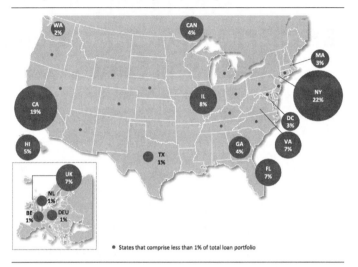

Blackstone's real estate eggs aren't all in one basket
BXMT's portfolio diversification by state/country

● States that comprise less than 1% of total loan portfolio

Source: Blackstone Mortgage Group

Those loans are spread across a large variety of property types. At last count, over 53% of its loans were for office space with 15% in hotels. Retail properties—probably one of the riskiest loan segments right now—account for just 8% of BXMT's total.

It's important to keep in mind that unlike a lot of REITs, BXMT doesn't own a lot of property itself. Instead, it loans money to other people looking to buy property. If for some reason those clients fail to keep up with their payments, BXMT can foreclose on the property.

Obviously, this is a last-ditch resort, and it's where the REIT's connection to the Blackstone Group comes in handy. Blackstone Real Estate has vast amounts of data on the real estate market, which is a big help for making solid lending decisions. This gives Blackstone Mortgage Trust a huge competitive advantage and is probably the reason that none of BXMT's loans is in default.

Blackstone Mortgage Trust manages its risk by lending only a conservative amount of cash compared with the value of the underlying properties.

The average loan-to-value ratio for Blackstone's portfolio is only 62%. In other words, on average, BXMT only lends $620,000 for every $1 million worth of property.

So even if a borrower stops paying on a particular loan, Blackstone can repossess the property and sell it for more than the actual loan amount. This way, Blackstone Mortgage Trust would be highly likely to recover the cash it lent to the borrower. In the worst-case scenario, it could end up with some very iconic properties.

Consider that in 2015, a real estate company borrowed $320 million from the Blackstone Mortgage Trust to pay down some debt it had at a higher interest rate. For collateral, they offered the iconic Woolworth Building, a historic skyscraper located in New York City.

At the time, the building was appraised at $470 million, meaning the loan represented just 68% of the property's value. So if the borrower had defaulted, BXMT would have taken possession of one of the most famous buildings in the Manhattan skyline . . . with a chance to make a significant profit by selling it.

In London, the company made a £78 million loan against the Aldwych House, a full 50% of what the building was appraised for. Its portfolio also includes a beachside resort in Maui, Hawaii. The $258 million loan is worth about 75% of the property's appraised value.

So BXMT is a great setup for investors. It earns interest on the money it lends. It also collects fees when a loan is made, and more fees if a loan is extended. If a loan goes into default, BXMT stands a good chance of recovering the loan and then some. And remember, as a REIT, the company must send at least 90% of its profits to shareholders.

Another thing that makes BXMT stand out is the type of loans that it makes. REITs often borrow money to fund new loans, and BXMT is no exception. The difference, though, is that most REITs lend at fixed interest rates while borrowing at floating rates.

In other words, the interest rate on the mortgage never changes while the interest rate the REIT is charged for borrowing the money can fluctuate. With interest rates slowly rising (and likely to accelerate under new Federal Reserve Chairman Jerome Powell), the REIT's loan costs will go up while the money it receives from its existing loans stays the same. That squeezes lending spreads and reduces profits.

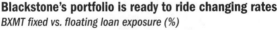

Blackstone's portfolio is ready to ride changing rates
BXMT fixed vs. floating loan exposure (%)

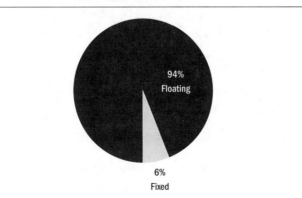

94%
Floating

6%
Fixed

Source: Blackstone Mortgage Group

BXMT doesn't have this problem because the majority of its loans have adjustable (floating) rates. That means that as rates rise, Blackstone's lending profits increase.

This makes BXMT's earnings fairly stable. So not surprisingly, its dividend payments are fairly stable, too.

BXMT's dividend payouts are fairly predictable

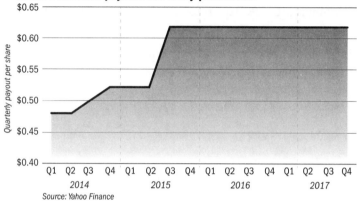

Source: Yahoo Finance

Let's see how the company stacks up to our Three Pillars.

Capital preservation: You can tell that Blackstone Mortgage Trust is focused on risk management given its 62% loan-to-value ratio. If a loan doesn't work out, chances are that Blackstone can easily recover the cash that was lent. But with 100% of its loans currently performing, default isn't a huge worry. These are disciplined lenders.

Growth: There are a couple ways that Blackstone's income and dividends can grow. The first is that Blackstone should continue to successfully lend money and grow its retained earnings. That means that over time, the loan portfolio will grow and so will earnings. The second is if interest rates rise, Blackstone is perfectly positioned to increase the bottom line. So while the dividend tends to be fairly stable, the company could look to increase its payout rates.

Yield: Since launching as Blackstone Mortgage Trust in 2013, the company's yield has gone from 4.2% to as high as 9.2%. As of the end of 2017, it was sitting at a comfortable 7.7%. This is an equity-like return just through the dividend alone. Share price appreciation can be the cherry on top of that.

Of course, the real draw for me is its close relationship with the Blackstone Group. This REIT offers steady payouts from the company's proven management style while we hope to see bigger and better payouts with the Blackstone Group's more opportunistic dividend.

Action to take: Consider buying shares of Blackstone Mortgage Trust (BXMT).

Blackstone Mortgage Trust trades under the symbol BXMT. As a REIT, its tax identification number is less important, since your paperwork will come directly from your broker. But just for the sake of completeness, it's 94-6181186.

CHAPTER 8:
GET PAID WELL WHILE TAKING A RISK

Like Blackstone Mortgage Trust, **Annaly Capital Management (NLY)** has a fairly simple business model. It buys mortgages from banks and other institutions and then generates profits from the payments the individual homeowners make on their mortgages.

From a very basic standpoint, it profits from a spread between interest rates. It uses its strong connections and excellent financial position to borrow money at low rates. Then it uses that capital to purchase mortgages that pay a higher rate of interest.

Now, there are a lot of subtleties that go into this business. Annaly must determine various levels of risk, such as how likely homeowners are to pay back their mortgages early (which will reduce the profit Annaly can capture). The company must also deal with fluctuating rates both on the financing side (what the company pays to borrow capital) and on the lending side (what homeowners are paying for their mortgages). Believe me, you don't want me to go into all of the specifics in this area.

However, some investors have worried whether Annaly can stay at the top of its game. Up until President Trump was elected, the Federal Reserve made glacial changes to interest rates with plenty of warning. That gave Annaly's team time to adjust.

But Federal Reserve Chairman Jerome Powell has promised to be much more aggressive with the country's monetary policy. Annaly may have to adjust faster than it has before. Failure to keep up with the changes could knock its bottom line.

I'm not too worried, though. Annaly is one of the best in the business when it comes to managing interest rate risk. In fact, back in 2015, when the Federal Reserve started raising interest rates again, the company began closing out some of its mortgage investments and paying off some of its borrowings. Reducing debt is a great tactical move to reduce the threat of rising interest rates. Debt becomes more expensive when interest rates increase.

Higher rates also give Annaly more opportunity to BUY mortgages when rates move higher. See, banks and other finance companies will likely panic once rates start rising—and sell their mortgages at cheap values (mortgages—like bonds—trade lower when rates move higher). When that happens, Annaly will have the ability to buy these mortgages at fire-sale prices, giving it (and us) great income investments at very attractive prices.

But here is where it gets really exciting. As of December 2017, the company's book value was $11.34 a share. That means if you sold everything the company owned and distributed it to shareholders, each share would be worth $11.34 each. Any share price below that could be considered a bargain.

Annaly spreads its risk by focusing on different industries
NLY's middle market lending portfolio by industry

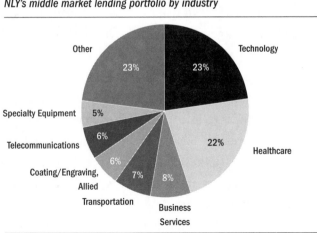

Source: Annaly Capital

The company has interests in a broad spectrum of real estate. The bulk of its money is agency debt, that is, mortgages backed by government agencies like Fannie Mae, Freddie Mac and Ginnie Mae. It essentially means the U.S. government is on the hook for making sure Annaly gets paid, which is a good position to be in.

It also has ties to residential credit markets, commercial real estate and middle market lending, which provides financing to private companies—that is, smaller startups that don't trade on regulated exchanges. These companies operate in a diverse range of industries, from technology to transportation. And no one industry makes up more than a quarter of Annaly's portfolio, which spreads out its risk.

Together, its business lines bring in lots of cash—much of which ends up in shareholders' pockets. Since its debut on the stock market in 1997, Annaly has steadily increased its payouts, paying out a total of $16 billion over a 20-year period.

Annaly has paid over $16 billion in dividends
NLY total payouts (millions $)

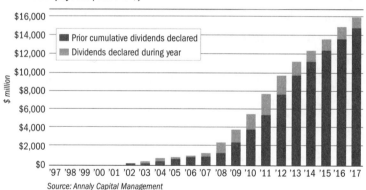

Legend: ■ Prior cumulative dividends declared / ▥ Dividends declared during year

Source: Annaly Capital Management

There's nothing an income investor loves more than a company that regularly boosts its payouts.

But at the same time, I want you to be aware of the risks associated with this position. As interest rates fluctuate over the next few years, it will be important for Annaly to balance its funding costs with its mortgage income. This requires foresight, discipline and timing.

Annaly has an experienced team that should be able to navigate this period very well. But you should still use caution when buying shares and not take too big of a position. The company's tremendous dividend yield should help drive the stock sharply higher in time, but there may be some turbulence along the way.

Capital preservation: Annaly has a smart management team that has built the company into one of the leading mortgage-based REITs. The bulk of its holdings are backed by the U.S. government, which is great for my confidence.

Growth: As I explained, this is the big question mark. The company's growth will depend on how well it navigates changing interest rates. It made all the right moves when the Fed started reversing course in 2015, but Powell may not be as patient or methodical. While I trust Annaly will continue to do well, know there is a risk its management may not play the current environment correctly.

Yield: Backstopping any fears about Annaly's business model is its commitment to making sure its shareholders get paid. It continued to increase payouts even during the financial crisis of 2008–09, which is just further proof of management's skill to handle tough situations.

So this is a risky one, but a risk I think worth taking.

Action to take: Consider buying shares of Annaly Capital Management (NLY).

Annaly Capital Management trades under the symbol NLY. Its tax identification number is 22-3479661.

CHAPTER 9:

HOW TO OWN A STAKE IN A BOND VILLAIN'S LAIR

Somewhere in rural Pennsylvania is a very special mountain. It's surrounded by armed guards and barbed wire. Beyond them is a road that disappears into the mountain itself—a 25-foot-high corridor that descends 22 stories into the earth.

The complex encompasses 145 acres and offers 55 million total square feet of space, all of it underground. It contains seven miles of roads and two miles of railroad tunnels to help people get around.

It might sound like something out of a James Bond movie, in which a bald man with an eye patch plots to take over the world. But it's actually just one of the properties owned by a very unique REIT: **Iron Mountain (IRM)**.

Iron Mountain is a secure storage company. It owns and operates facilities where clients can keep their most treasured possessions—from physical items to important data.

Its facility in Butler County, Pennsylvania, was once a limestone mine. Today it holds everything from the original copies of classic motion pictures and priceless original photographs of Abraham Lincoln to essential data for over 2,300 corporations and government agencies.

And while that all sounds cool, there's really nothing too flashy about what Iron Mountain does. It gives companies a place to store documents and data safely. With the world becoming more dangerous and corporate data becoming more vulnerable, companies see the value in having someplace to keep tax information, purchase and sale receipts, disaster recovery documents, legal records, health documents and more. We are talking about both physical and data backup for electronic files.

Source: BizJournals.com

Iron Mountain is the largest provider of these services on the planet, operating in 53 countries on six different continents. It provides a safe and organized location for document storage. It also offers related services such as document pickup and delivery, shredding and disposal and records management for regulatory purposes.

This is a business with staying power, having originally been founded in an underground facility near Hudson, New York, way back in 1951. Across the 53 countries in which it now operates, Iron Mountain has 230,000 customers in industries such as legal, financial, health care, insurance, life sciences, energy, entertainment and government. All told, 95% of the companies in the Fortune 1000 are customers.

While Iron Mountain has been around since 1951, it experienced very rapid growth over the past 20 years. In 1996 the company operated 6 million square feet across 85 facilities. At last count, those numbers had grown to 87 million square feet and 1,433 facilities.

The company believes that it still has plenty of growth ahead of it given that in-house storage still represents the majority of global information management. That means there are lots of additional potential customers who could benefit from Iron Mountain's services. That is particularly true in emerging economies, where this industry is just getting started.

Iron Mountain's revenues are obviously primarily based on renting storage space to a large, diverse base of customers. Those revenues are topped off with fees from the other related services that the company provides. Here's a quick look at its main business lines:

Secure storage: This is the company's largest source of revenue and involves providing nondedicated storage rental space to customers for key data storage. Nondedicated space means that customers can increase or decrease how much space they use at any given time.

No single customer accounted for more than 1% of the company's secure storage revenue in 2017. The secure off-site storage of data backup is a key component of every company's disaster recovery and business continuity plans, which means that Iron Mountain is providing an essential service.

Physical records storage: Iron Mountain provides a safe place for companies to store their inactive records—files that aren't needed for immediate access but have to be retained for legal, compliance or regulatory reasons.

Electronic records storage: Iron Mountain stores computer tapes, cartridges and disk packs in climate-controlled facilities, where they are available to customers 24 hours a day, 365 days of the year. Iron Mountain's storage is not connected to the internet and therefore provides superior protection against data breaches and hacks, obviously something of huge importance today.

Service offerings: Iron Mountain offers to physically handle and transport records as necessary as well as destroy them upon expiration of retention periods. Iron Mountain's courier fleet consists of 4,500 owned or leased vehicles. When it comes to destroying unneeded records, it can use old-fashioned shredding as well as offer secure information technology asset destruction.

Together, these business segments generate durable, low-volatility growth throughout every kind of economic cycle. For one thing, the majority of the company's revenues are from fixed monthly storage rental fees. Once a customer places physical records with Iron Mountain, IRM will generate fees until those records are destroyed or removed (for which Iron Mountain charges a fee). Similarly, contracts for the storage of electronic backup involve fixed monthly rental payments.

For an idea of how long a customer tends to stick with Iron Mountain, check out the chart below. It shows that 50% of the boxes stored with Iron Mountain remain with the company and are still generating revenue 15 years later. A quarter of boxes are still around 22 years later. It's hard to think of another business with similar retention rates.

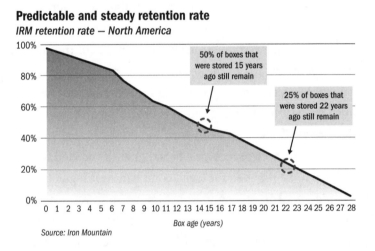

Predictable and steady retention rate
IRM retention rate — North America

Source: Iron Mountain

Because of that loyalty, Iron Mountain typically doesn't experience significant reductions in storage rental revenue during recessions or economic downturns. It just makes sense. Once a company has outsourced this service and eliminated any headcount and infrastructure that had been in place for providing in-house storage, they aren't going to reverse course and add people plus facilities during a downturn.

The opposite is also true, though. This business isn't going to soar during an economic boom either, at least not from its regular customers. But it's counting on its clients in North America to provide slow, steady growth in the years ahead while it looks for opportunities to grow even faster in key emerging markets.

Much of that growth in emerging markets is going to involve Iron Mountain making accretive acquisitions of smaller businesses. As the

800-pound gorilla in this industry, Iron Mountain can achieve efficiencies of scale that smaller competitors can't. For example, in December 2017 Iron Mountain acquired a similar company in India, laying the groundwork for growth in that huge country. By 2020, it expects 25% of its business to be growing in emerging markets, up from 20% at the end of 2016.

The downside of going on an acquisition bender is that we might have to settle for lower dividends in the short term. The company is committed to dividend growth, however, so it will be very reluctant to cut payouts if it can be avoided. Plus, as it opens up shop in growing markets, it will earn more cash to use to reward shareholders.

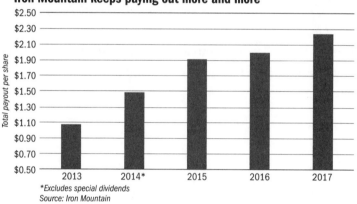

Iron Mountain keeps paying out more and more

*Excludes special dividends
Source: Iron Mountain

It's already done a good job sending money to investors. The company restructured itself as a REIT in 2014, leading to a big jump in its payouts. And it occasionally pays out bonus dividends when events warrant.

Let's see how it looks under the Three Pillars microscope.

Capital preservation: Iron Mountain has a huge competitive moat. A potential competitor would need to invest billions and billions of dollars to even match the company's capabilities. Further, Iron Mountain's future cash flows are extremely predictable given its incredible customer retention rates. This is a predictable, reliable business built on a sound financial foundation.

Growth: Iron Mountain is not a revolutionary technology company. So the short-term growth here is not going to knock your socks off. But the long term is a very different story. This company just keeps growing year after year after year, and the inroads it's making into foreign markets could boost its returns.

Yield: As a REIT, the company must pay out most of its profits to shareholders. Its quest to acquire companies in foreign countries could take a bite out of those profits. Still, management aims to grow its dividend by 5% in 2018 and by 4% a year until 2020. Those are modest but achievable goals.

Since 1951, Iron Mountain has steadily built a giant, cash-flowing business with a major competitive moat around it. It is a business that is still steadily growing, with great long-term opportunities ahead.

And with so many top-notch clients, you can bet there are plenty of senators and congressmen collecting checks from the company. I suggest you join them.

Action to take: Consider buying shares of Iron Mountain (IRM).

Iron Mountain trades under the stock symbol IRM. Its tax identification number is 23-2588479.

CHAPTER 10:

HOW TO "TAX BACK" THE U.S. GOVERNMENT

"In this world, nothing can be said to be certain, except death and taxes."

Those words are as true today as when Benjamin Franklin wrote them in 1789. Even with the Tax Cuts and Jobs Act of 2017, you're still going to send a nice chunk of change to Uncle Sam every year.

The "Congressional Checks" I've been telling you about will take away some of that sting—letting you cash in on the rules politicians added to the law to enrich themselves. But this next opportunity takes it a step further.

You can think of it as a way to get a rebate on the money Washington takes from you, or as an opportunity to collect taxes from the U.S. government.

It takes advantage of the fact that the U.S. government is the world's largest employer—with a total of 4.2 million employees. Take out the military and you still have 2.7 million federal workers—more employees than Walmart or McDonald's has worldwide.

All of those employees need a place to work, so you'd probably expect the government to own a bunch of office buildings for them. After all, the federal government owns nearly 640 million acres of land . . . about 28% of the total land area in the United States.

But the truth is that the federal government turns to the private sector for a lot of its office needs, renting space from somebody else just like a business. At last count, it was leasing over 55,000 properties. Remember, this is the government we're talking about—it doesn't necessarily rent efficiently. With plenty of taxpayer cash available, government employees don't often worry about how much is paid in rent.

Government rental contracts typically stay in place, locking in long-term leases. Plus, these agencies typically pay rent on time. So if we want to collect a portion of that rent, we have to turn to the private-sector companies the government uses to find offices for its employees. My favorite company in this space is **Government Properties Income Trust (GOV)**, a REIT that is also the U.S. government's largest landlord.

While there are other real estate companies with U.S. government tenants, GOV focuses mostly on getting government business. It leases office space to agencies such as U.S. Immigration and Customs, the FBI, the CDC, the FDA and the Department of Homeland Security as well as many state agencies.

Just check out the complete list below:

Tenant list

TENANT	RENTABLE SQ. FT	% OF TOTAL RENTABLE SQ. FT.	% OF ANNUALIZED RENTAL INCOME
U.S. Government:			
1. U.S Customs & Immigration Service	718,169	6.7%	11.6%
2. Internal Revenue Service	1,041,806	9.7%	8.7%
3. U.S. Government	406,388	3.8%	5.0%
4. Federal Bureau of Investigation	304,257	2.8%	3.5%
5. Department of Justice	221,701	2.1%	3.1%
6. Department of Veterans Affairs	295,172	2.8%	2.9%
7. Centers for Disease Control	297,890	2.7%	2.5%
8. Defence Intelligence Agency	266,000	2.5%	2.2%
9. Department of Homeland Security	125,153	1.2%	2.0%
10. Social Security Administration	189,645	1.8%	1.9%
11. National Business Center	212,996	2.0%	1.9%
12. National Park Service	166,745	1.6%	1.9%
13. Department of Energy	220,702	2.1%	1.9%
14. U.S. Courts	115,366	1.1%	1.8%
15. Natural Resource Center	150,551	1.4%	1.5%
16. Department of Health and Human Services	128,645	1.2%	1.4%
17. Drug Enforcement Agency	147,955	1.4%	1.3%
18. National Archives and Record Administration	352,064	3.3%	1.3%
19. Bureau of Land Management	154,280	1.5%	1.1%

20. Department of State	89,058	0.8%	1.1%
21. U.S. Postal Service	321,800	3.0%	1.0%
22. Defense Nuclear Facilities Board	58,931	0.6%	1.0%
23. Occupational Health and Safety Administration	57,770	0.5%	0.9%
24. Military Entrance Processing Station	56,931	0.5%	0.8%
25. Financial Management Service	87,993	0.8%	0.8%
26. Centers for Medicare and Medicaid Services	78,361	0.7%	0.8%
27. Department of Housing and Urban Development	88,559	0.8%	0.7%
28. Environmental Protection Agency	43,232	0.4%	0.6%
29. Department of the Army	228,108	2.1%	0.6%
30. Food and Drug Administration	33,398	0.3%	0.4%
31. Department of Defense	31,030	0.3%	0.3%
32. Bureau of Prisons	51,138	0.5%	0.3%
33. Equal Employment Opportunity Commission	19,409	0.2%	0.2%
34. Small Business Administration	8,575	0.1%	0.1%
35. Executive Office for Immigration Review	5,500	0.1%	0.1%
36. Non Government	10,080	0.1%	0.1%
37. Department of Labor	6,459	0.1%	0.0%
Subtotal U.S. Government	6,781,817	63.5%	67.0%

TENANT	RENTABLE SQ. FT	% OF TOTAL RENTABLE SQ. FT.	% OF ANNUALIZED RENTAL INCOME
State Government:			
1. State of California — six agency occupants	416,852	3.9%	4.2%
2. Commonwealth of Massachusetts — three agency occupants	307,119	2.9%	4.0%
3. Commonwealth of Virginia — seven agency occupants	255,241	2.4%	2.3%
4. State of Georgia — Department of Transportation	293,035	2.7%	2.3%
5. State of New Jersey — one agency occupant	173,189	1.6%	1.9%
6. State of Oregon — two agency occupants	199,018	1.9%	1.9%
7. State of Washington — Social and Health Services	111,908	1.0%	1.1%
8. State of Arizona — Northern Arizona University	66,743	0.6%	0.6%
9. State of Maryland — two agency occupants	84,674	0.8%	0.5%
10. State of South Carolina — four agency occupants	121,561	0.8%	0.5%
11. State of Minnesota — Minnesota State Lottery	61,426	1.1%	0.5%
12. State of New York — Department of Agriculture	64,000	0.6%	0.4%
Subtotal State Government	2,154,766	20.1%	20.3%
The United Nations	187,060	1.7%	4.5%
Municipalities	111,595	1.0%	1.0%
146 Non-Government Tenants	879,763	8.2%	7.2%
Subtotal Leased Rentable Square Feet	10,115,001	94.5%	100.0%
Available for Lease	585,963	5.5%	—
Total Rentable Square Feet	10,700,964	100.0%	100.0%

These are agencies that ensure the well-being of the United States and have some of the largest budgets aside from the U.S. military. Big-budget tenants are a great thing if you are a landlord—you can always expect rent when it's due.

The company leases office space to state governments as well. In all, it owns 74 properties spread across 31 states and the District of Columbia. See all the shaded states in the map below? That's where you'll find properties owned by GOV.

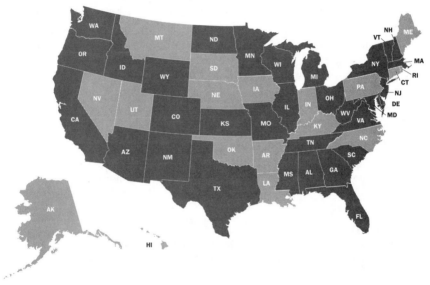

Source: Government Properties Income Trust

Every day, thousands of government workers file into one of GOV's properties to do their jobs. Every month, GOV collects rent payments for each of these properties. And since GOV is a REIT, it sends a large portion of its profits back to shareholders every quarter. At last count, it paid a steady dividend of 43 cents a share every three months, giving the stock a yield over 12%.

So with GOV, you're essentially creating an income loop for yourself. You pay taxes to the government. The government uses that money to pay rent to GOV. Then each quarter, GOV sends a portion of that money back to you!

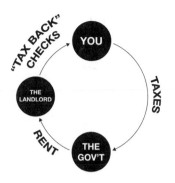

Here's how it looks in our Three Pillars.

Capital preservation: GOV is always on the hunt for new opportunities, and its acquisitions can sometimes be costly. Pessimistic investors tend to dump the stock when they think the company is spending too much money. On the other hand, GOV has plenty of big government agencies locked into long-term contracts, and it can sell real estate if it happens to get into trouble. So while the stock price can get volatile, I think it's ultimately a safe play.

Growth: There's a good reason GOV goes on acquisition binges—to buy new growth. I expect their new properties to pay off, delivering even greater profits. Another potential stumbling block is President Trump's mission to make government smaller and more efficient. You'd expect the real estate magnate to take a critical eye to long-term leases. Of course, Trump is learning that restructuring the government is harder than he thought. Besides, even if the federal government starts scaling back, state governments will need to start filling in the gaps. So GOV should land on its feet.

Yield: GOV has a habit of paying a steady dividend, no matter what its balance sheet looks like. Of course, it would be great if GOV regularly boosted its payouts. But there's nothing wrong with getting regular, predictable checks.

Of all the opportunities I've told you about so far, this is probably the least dynamic of them all. Its growth path is a little rocky, and its dividend growth isn't anything to write home about. Still, the fact that it takes in tax dollars and sends them out to investors melds nicely with the whole

"Congressional Check" idea. So I think it will make a fine—if boring—addition to your portfolio.

Action to take: Consider buying shares of Government Properties Income Trust (GOV).

Government Properties Income Trust trades under the symbol GOV. Its tax identification number is 26-4273474.

CHAPTER 11:
LET JEFF BEZOS WRITE YOU SOME CHECKS

A lot of REITs operate retail properties—malls, storefronts, shopping centers and the like. And there's a good reason you won't find many of them in this book. It's called the retail apocalypse.

For over a decade, retail stores have suffered from falling sales. But in 2017, things hits a major tipping point. Household names like Sears, Macy's and J.C. Penney individually announced over 100 closings of retail outlets. At least 19 companies declared bankruptcy, including iconic names like Toys R Us and RadioShack.

You don't have to think too hard to figure out why. People have just gotten used to the convenience of buying things online. Why fight traffic, search for parking and wander through a store when you can find everything you need on the internet and have it delivered straight to your house?

And of course, the No. 1 company that's leading customers away from brick-and-mortar stores is Amazon.com. Jeff Bezos founded the company in 1994 to sell books. But it quickly spread into new markets, taking business away from more and more retail stores.

Not only are the retailers suffering, but so are the REITs that depend on the rental income from the retailers.

If a retail-based REIT wants to survive the carnage, it will have to manage its business more carefully. That's why I recommend checking out

National Retail Properties (NNN). Despite its name, the company has developed a strategy to avoid the retail apocalypse. It even counts Amazon as one of its clients—meaning some of the money you collect from it will be coming from Jeff Bezos' pocket.

National Retail is a highly diversified landlord with over 400 different tenants who lease a combined 2,543 properties. The company's leases have a long average duration of more than 11.7 years, and the business is fully focused on the United States.

National retail's widely diversified real estate portfolio
Geographic distribution of tenants

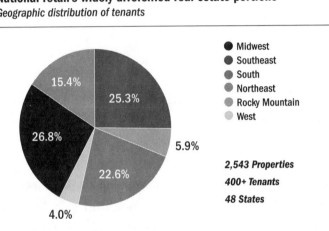

- Midwest
- Southeast
- South
- Northeast
- Rocky Mountain
- West

2,543 Properties
400+ Tenants
48 States

Source: National Retail Properties

More importantly, more than 95% of its tenants are in businesses that can't be easily usurped by online competition. I'm talking about convenience stores, restaurants, automotive service, fitness centers and movie theaters. As long as people buy gas, eat out or head to the gym, National Retail's clients will be largely immune to the retail apocalypse. Take a look at its full list of tenants on the next page.

Included in that list are dominant brands like 7-Eleven, Wendy's, Dairy Queen, PetSmart, Starbucks, Citibank, Taco Bell and Bank of America. Another one of the National Retail's many tenants is Whole Foods, the grocery store chain that Amazon picked up in 2017. Essentially, Amazon is paying rent to National Retail.

National retail's Amazon-proof tenant base
Industry and tenant base of national retail

Line of trade	% of base rent	# of properties	# of tenants	# of states
1. Convenience stores	16.8%	504	52	28
2. Restaurants – full service	11.7%	413	81	38
3. Restaurants – limited service	7.5%	352	70	33
4. Automotive service	7.0%	209	13	26
5. Family entertainment centers	6.1%	91	4	25
6. Health and fitness	5.7%	35	7	17
7. Theaters	4.9%	30	5	15
8. Automotive parts	3.8%	180	4	35
9. RV dealers, parts and accessories	3.4%	32	1	19
10. Banks	2.7%	114	5	9
11. Sporting goods	2.5%	15	4	13
12. Medical service providers	2.4%	78	18	18
13. Wholesale clubs	2.3%	8	1	4
14. Drug stores	2.1%	39	4	17
15. Consumer electronics	1.9%	20	2	13
16. Home improvements	1.9%	24	10	12
17. Travel plazas	1.9%	28	6	8
18. Furniture	1.9%	42	17	22
19. General merchandise	1.8%	59	14	21
20. Home furnishings	1.7%	18	6	13
Other	10.0%	252	100	40
Total	100.0%	2,543		

Source: National Retail Properties

You'll find these stores in high-traffic locations, making them valuable real estate. It's one of the reasons National Retail has great occupancy rates, meaning most of their properties have rent-paying tenants. The chart on the next page shows how National Retail's ability to keep its properties rented stacks up against the rest of the REIT industry.

As you can see, from 2003–2017, National Retail's average occupancy rate has been 97.9%, never dipping below 96.4%. Those lows came during the 2008–09 financial crisis, when the average REIT was struggling to keep 90% of their buildings profitable.

National retail properties superior occupancy rates
Annual occupancy percentage rate

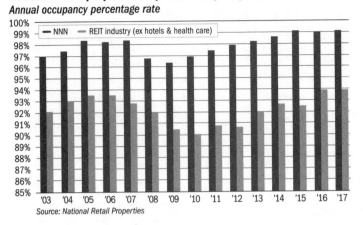

Source: National Retail Properties

National Retail owes its superior occupancy performance to carefully selecting tenants involved in stable businesses and focusing on easily rentable Main Street properties with reasonable rental rates. And every one of those contracts has annual rental increases built into them, ensuring regular revenue growth. It's a strategy that has literally paid dividends for decades, as you can see in the chart below:

An exceptional track record of dividend growth
Annual dividend per share — National Retail Properties

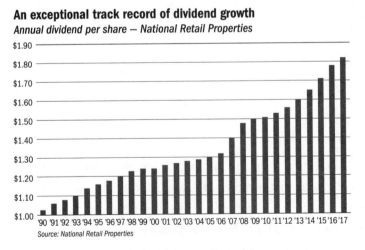

Source: National Retail Properties

Let's see how it stacks up to our Three Pillars.

Capital Preservation: National Retail has one of the best balance sheets in the REIT sector. Its average lease term of 11.7 years provides great visibility on future cash flows. The company's prime real estate locations provide even further comfort should some of its tenants leave. It sailed through the Great Recession and has positioned itself to avoid the retail apocalypse.

Growth: As a whole, real estate provides steady and predictable growth. Over time, the value of National Retail's properties will increase, as will the cash flow that those properties generate and the amount of the dividend that the company can pay. And remember, annual rent increases are built into all of National Retail's contracts with tenants.

Yield: National Retail has had 27 consecutive years of dividend increases—something very few companies can match. Combine that growth with a yield of this size and I think the company could be a big long-term winner for you.

In short, this REIT isn't just immune to the Amazon-induced retail apocalypse—it's also profiting from Amazon. And with a solid record of paying more and more money to shareholders, this is a great company to own.

Action to take: Consider buying shares of National Retail Properties (NNN).

National Retail Properties trades under the symbol NNN. Its IRS tax number is 56-1431377.

CHAPTER 12:
LOCK IN A BIG DIVIDEND WITH THIS LOCKUP REIT

Lots of REITs own and operate properties that people want to go to, from state-of-the-art office buildings to luxury hotels. But our next REIT specializes in properties that no one wants to spend any time in.

CoreCivic (CXW) owns and operates American prisons and detention centers. It was founded in 1983 under the name Corrections Corp. of America. In 1984, it became the first U.S. company to be awarded a government prison contract, overseeing a corrections facility in Tennessee.

Today it competes with another company called GEO Group for the title of largest private corrections company. Judged by the number of beds it owns, CoreCivic has the crown locked down. All told, it owns 82 facilities and manages seven other sites in government partnerships.

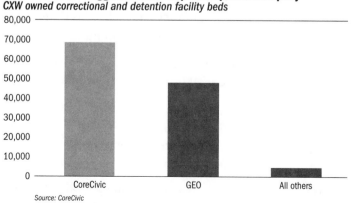

CoreCivic is the biggest American private prison company
CXW owned correctional and detention facility beds

Source: CoreCivic

The company earns revenue from long-term contracts with various federal, state and local agencies that rent space and services in their facilities. The business appeals to government entities for several reasons:

- Private companies can design and construct a new correctional facility in half the time a comparable government project can, often for half the price
- Governments can reduce or share their liability exposure by contracting with private corrections companies
- Private companies have labor, administration and operation costs 20% less than those of public institutions
- Private companies offer state-of-the-art correctional facility designs that are more efficient
- Private companies reduce the pressures and costs of overcrowding in the public prison system.

The business is broken into three main business areas. Its Safety division oversees the company's prisons. At last count, its properties had over 64,000 beds. Not all of this business is watching over hardened criminals, though. It also has contracts with the U.S. Immigration and Customs Enforcement (ICE) agency to house illegal aliens during processing.

The company's Property division builds and renovates detention facilities and then leases them to other entities. Again, this solves a major government problem when it comes to prison construction. It can build new facilities faster and cheaper than the government can. And by leasing them, it is responsible for maintaining the property, too.

Perhaps the most interesting CoreCivic division is Community. It owns and operates halfway houses, facilities to help former prisoners re-enter the world. This includes providing job training, therapy, substance abuse programs and more. Essentially, the company is working to reduce prison populations.

Across all three of these business units, CoreCivic has 125 agreements with federal, state and local agencies. That's a great level of diversity, which helps spread the company's risk nicely. If one of these states were to suddenly cut ties with CoreCivic, its revenues wouldn't take a big hit.

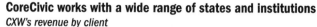

CoreCivic works with a wide range of states and institutions
CXW's revenue by client

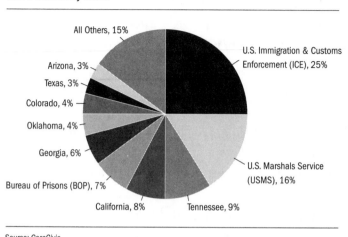

All Others, 15%

Arizona, 3%

Texas, 3%

Colorado, 4%

Oklahoma, 4%

Georgia, 6%

Bureau of Prisons (BOP), 7%

California, 8%

Tennessee, 9%

U.S. Immigration & Customs Enforcement (ICE), 25%

U.S. Marshals Service (USMS), 16%

Source: CoreCivic

The only real exception to that idea is its contracts with ICE, which represent 25% of CoreCivic's revenue. Ordinarily, counting on a single customer for such a large chunk of your business is something to worry about. But with President Trump's focus on immigration enforcement, the fact that ICE dominates CoreCivic's balance sheet doesn't seem like too much of a risk to me.

Of course, prisons tend to be a touchy subject, and CoreCivic has seen its share of controversies. That's likely the reason its security contracts tend to be short term, usually no more than five years with optional extensions. It gives the politicians flexibility to break with the company in case the political winds shift.

In fact, in 2016, the U.S. Justice Department recommended that the U.S. Bureau of Prisons should stop using private prisons. As you'd expect, that caused a huge dip in CoreCivic's share price. It started to rebound when the department reversed its stance in February 2017. A leaked memo specifically directed the agency to increase "population levels in private contract facilities."

Another potential cause of concern is falling crime rates in the United States and the resulting drop in prison populations. According to the most recent numbers, the prison population in 2016 was down 1% from 2015 and down 7% from its height in 2009.

But I can't imagine crime will ever entirely go away, and the Justice Department's newfound love of private prisons is just the beginning. In March 2018, Kentucky's state budget allotted more funding for private prisons.

If more state governments come around to the idea, or if ICE wants to expand their ability to detail illegal aliens, CoreCivic has a ready solution standing by. Its portfolio has seven idle facilities with the potential to hold nearly 10,000 inmates. One is in Texas and another is in New Mexico, meaning they're right where ICE would want them if there's a stronger immigration countdown.

But even if the political winds do shift, there's plenty of potential in CoreCivic's Community division. After all, we can't lock up every criminal and throw away the key. According to CoreCivic, 95% of prisoners in state prisons are eventually released and 75% or so are eventually arrested again. Politicians from both sides of the aisle can agree that if an inmate is released from prison, steps should be taken to prevent him or her from becoming a repeat offender.

To that end, CoreCivic has spent $300 million to build its portfolio of halfway houses. It bought eight such facilities in 2017, spending a total of $45.6 million to acquire them. It is now the second-largest provider of prisoner "re-entry" services in the United States.

Remember, states and the feds pay CoreCivic for these services, meaning the company gets money to keep people in jail as well as out of jail. And as a REIT, CoreCivic returns a large portion of its earnings to shareholders.

The company paid $2.16 a share in 2015 and 2016 before lowering the dividend in 2017. Usually, a decision to decrease the dividend is a huge red flag. But in this case, the company was anticipating lower profits because of the Justice Department's stance on private prisons. Plus, it needed extra money to fund its acquisitions of halfway houses.

That comes across as a very smart move to me. Keeping shareholders happy with high dividends is great, as long as the payouts aren't reckless.

And with the Justice Department's new directive to contract with private prisons, not to mention Donald Trump's fixation on going after people in the country illegally, I expect CoreCivic will soon have plenty of reasons to boost its payouts.

And don't forget about its Properties division. Building and leasing prisons is a lot less controversial than running them. In fact, governments are much more willing to sign longer-term contracts in this area. All 12 of its properties are fully leased. And in January 2018 it signed an agreement to build a new correctional facility in Kansas, which Kansas will then lease for 20 years. And here's what it looks like:

So there's a lot to like here beyond its core business of owning private prisons. Let's put the company through our Three Pillars wringer.

Capital preservation: Before Donald Trump was elected, it looked like the pendulum was swinging against the idea of private prisons. That's why CoreCivic wisely expanded its operations into other incarceration-related areas. With Trump in office, prospects for private prisons are looking up, and CoreCivic has fostered a close relationship with ICE, boosting its prospects as crackdowns on illegal aliens increase. I just don't see any downsides in the near future, and if there are, I trust CoreCivic's management to adjust to them.

Growth: Some politicians believe more incarceration is the key to solving crime in America. Others believe it's rehabilitation. CoreCivic caters to both schools of thought, allowing politicians to fight crime without putting a strain on budgets. And as Congress continues to drag its feet on immigration reform, I expect CoreCivic's contracts with ICE will only deliver more and more profits.

Yield: As I mentioned, CoreCivic cut its dividend in 2017, mostly to fund acquisitions in preparation of the Justice Department moving away from private prisons. The company still pays an excellent yield, however, and there are plenty of reasons to expect that payout to increase.

Now, I recognize this will be a controversial recommendation because it touches on so many hot-button issues. But from a strict investor's point of view, there's a lot to like here. CoreCivic found an excellent niche for itself. And when that niche was threatened, it expanded its operations to tap new markets. All the while, it's paid a better-than-average dividend.

So I'm comfortable recommending that you add this company's "Congressional Checks" to your portfolio.

Action to take: Consider buying shares of CoreCivic (CXW).

CoreCivic trades under the symbol CXW. Its tax identification number is 62-1763875.

CHAPTER 13:
GET YOUR SHARE OF RISING HEALTH CARE COSTS

Our final three opportunities have a few traits in common.

First, they're all REITs, which means they pay the kinds of checks that politicians voted to cut taxes on. Second, they specialize in a certain industry—one that often finds itself mired in political controversy. And finally, they focus on properties that people ordinarily don't like to visit.

You might think I'm talking about more prisons, like the kind CoreCivic runs. But in this case, I'm talking about medical facilities—everything from major hospitals to local doctor's offices.

Unlike businesses that can be opened in just about any retail space, hospitals and the like require special considerations. They're subject to health codes more stringent than anything even restaurants have to deal with. Even things like the sizes of their doors must meet certain standards.

Depending on what the office does, allowances have to be made for storing radioactive materials, powerful drugs and even things contaminated with, er, biological matter. Then there's all the specialized equipment that needs exotic hookups. Even a dentist's office in a strip mall is more specialized than a bookstore or frozen yogurt shop. Your dentist needs complicated water setups, protection from X-rays and more.

So if ever there were an area for REITs to thrive, this would be it. They can take on the risks and costs of building, operating and maintaining buildings that meet doctors' exacting needs. In return, it gets regular rent checks from the doctors.

This essentially means we're getting paid thanks to health care costs, a topic that has dominated headlines ever since President Obama launched his plan to "fix" our medical system. Of course, those efforts have largely failed, and no one from either political party can agree on a solution. That will likely mean ever-larger price increases for a long time to come.

Meanwhile, as you've no doubt heard, the American population is getting older and living longer. The U.S. Census Bureau estimates there are currently 51 million Americans over the age of 65. By 2050, there could be as many as 88 million U.S. citizens over the age of 65. Meanwhile, the average life expectancy clocked in at under 79 years in 2015. A study published in *The Lancet* in 2017 expected that number to be up to over 81 years by 2030.

But longer lives require more effort to fight the effects of aging. According to the Centers for Medicare and Medicaid Services, national spending on health care is expected to rise 5.5% a year until 2026. Medicare spending will increase by 7.4% a year!

Of course, Medicare doesn't cover all of a senior's medical bills. And according to the Kaiser Family Foundation, aging Americans will need to spend up to half their Social Security checks to cover Medicare shortfalls by 2030.

Health care REITs will be one of the most obvious beneficiaries of this spending as the need for convenient and state-of-the-art facilities continues to grow. One of the biggest of the bunch, **HCP Inc. (HCP)**, will specifically benefit from the needs of aging seniors.

Founded in 1985, HCP has become the "go-to" spot for any hospital, clinic or assisted care business looking to open a new location. It owns 828 medical properties representing $18 billion of real estate. And the rent that HCP charges for these properties nets out to $1.8 billion each year.

The business is broken up into different areas of the health care industry. Just 7% of its properties are proper hospitals. It also holds a healthy number of doctor's offices, followed closely by "life sciences" facilities.

These are designed for medical research—everything from testing new drugs to conducting academic studies.

HCP covers a wide range of medical needs
HCP's holdings as a percentage of enterprise value

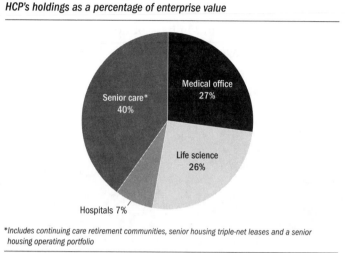

*Includes continuing care retirement communities, senior housing triple-net leases and a senior housing operating portfolio

Source: HCP, Inc.

The bulk of its assets are devoted to seniors. It owns nursing homes and retirement communities and some facilities that are a combination of both. In some cases it owns and operates the properties itself. It also rents out facilities it owns under what are known as triple-net leases. Under these agreements, the tenant pays all taxes and insurance fees for the property and is responsible for maintaining the property, too. That means HCP pretty much just collects rent checks.

Now, to be fair, the company has had a rough couple of years thanks to some business decisions that didn't quite pan out. In 2014 it expanded operations into the United Kingdom, only to start divesting itself from the country in 2018. It also had problems spinning off its line of skilled nursing facilities, which included rehabilitation centers and the like.

HCP's course corrections have adversely affected its earnings, as you'd probably expect. In 2016, the company drastically cut its dividend. As I mentioned earlier, that's usually a very bad sign. But as is the case with CoreCivic, I think it was the right move here.

The company is moving forward with plans to sell other underperforming assets. The sales will improve its balance sheet while giving it cash to spend on other projects. For instance, it's in a partnership to develop a luxury building for seniors in Seattle, Washington. The strategically located building offers multiple levels of care, essentially allowing seniors to stay where they are even as their health needs change.

It also recently started a third phase of development at a life science facility known as The Cove in San Francisco, California. The first two phases are fully leased, meaning HCP is not worried about idle space on the property. The company is also planning another life science project known as Sierra Point nearby.

The Cove (S. San Francisco)   Sierra Point (S. San Francisco)

It's a risky venture, to be sure. And considering the company's other missteps of the past few years, you might be a bit wary of putting your trust in it. So here's one more thing to think about.

The stock analysts at Morningstar took a close look at HCP's assets, considering their potential value and weighing them against the company's liabilities. By their math, the company has a net asset value of $31 a share. That is, if you divide their estimate of the company's true value among each of its shares, that's how much you get.

So in theory, any price below $31 a share makes HCP a bargain. And shares of HCP haven't traded above $31 since the summer of 2017! That means we have a nice floor of safety.

Here's how it looks in the Three Pillars.

Capital preservation: HCP's management has taken some missteps, which is reflected in the company's share price. But management has committed itself to selling underperforming assets and focusing on its core strengths. So you have a chance to buy in at a relatively inexpensive price right now. If nothing else, the fact that the company has an estimated net asset value of $31 should give you confidence if you buy shares below that price.

Growth: There's no doubt HCP is in a growth industry. Its slow shift to focus more on aging seniors should pay off in the years ahead. It also helps that they're clearing deadwood from their books. Buy in at a bargain price now and you could ride it higher as its restructuring bears fruit.

Yield: To income investors, a dividend cut is a real gut punch. It's even worse when you learn that up until 2016, HCP had a history of boosting its dividend every year since 2004. On the other hand, I respect the company for realizing its old rate was unsustainable. And if its plans work out the way I expect them too, we should see a return to higher dividends in the years ahead.

The bottom line is that America's health care costs aren't going to drop anytime soon, and HCP is poised to earn income from the demographic that will bear more and more of those costs. Yes, management made some mistakes but it seems to be back on track. I suggest buying shares before they're no longer a bargain.

Action to take: Consider buying shares of HCP Inc. (HCP).

HCP Inc. trades under the symbol HCP. Its tax identification number is 33-0091377.

CHAPTER 14:
THIS REIT COULD DOUBLE YOUR MONEY IN A DECADE

Continuing our health care theme is **Welltower (WELL)**.

The company was founded in Lima, Ohio, in 1970 with a pair of skilled nursing facilities. It was one of the first health care-related REITs to go public. Today it has interests in 1,279 properties across the U.S., Canada and the United Kingdom.

Over its long history, it's had to adjust to major shifts in the health care industry. Consider the rise of outpatient surgery. A decade or two ago, it would have been unthinkable to have surgery done anywhere but inside a hospital. Today, thousands of procedures can be performed outside of a hospital and the patient can recover in their own home.

That means fewer people are going to the hospital. According to the American Hospital Association, the number of people admitted to hospitals has been steadily declining since 2009. So like HCP, Welltower has shifted its business plan to match.

On the next page you can see how Welltower's property portfolio looked in 2010 and at the end of 2017.

As you'll see, the company's management essentially dumped its hospitals to expand into an area they see having more growth—senior care. It's going after this market even more aggressively than HCP is. In 2017 alone it sold over $3.3 billion worth of property, using the money to pay down debt and buy more senior housing projects.

Welltower's asset mix, 2010

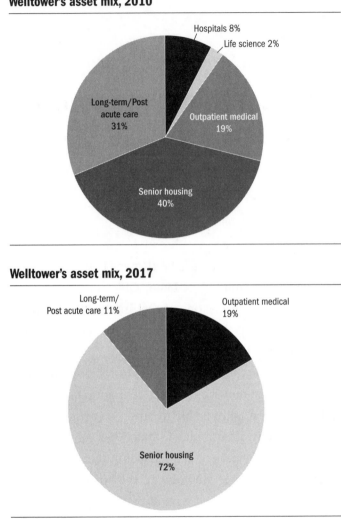

Welltower's asset mix, 2017

Source: Welltower

Welltower has entered into several joint ventures to manage these properties, but in a very smart way. A wise investor never puts all his eggs in one basket. So Welltower has spread its risk by working with a wide range of partners.

The largest is Sunrise Senior Living, which represents 36% of Welltower's operating income. If Sunrise were to get into financial trouble, Welltower would no doubt take a hit, too. But it would be even worse if Welltower counted on Sunrise for a larger portion of its revenue.

The company also spreads its risk by operating in several urban areas. The bulk of Welltower's 624 senior facilities in the United States are found in Los Angeles, Boston and New York. Its U.K. operations focus on Manchester, Birmingham and London. And not surprisingly, most of its Canadian facilities congregate around Toronto, Vancouver and Montreal.

The company has also adjusted how it gets paid, too. Back in 2010, 31% of its revenues came from public health care agencies like Medicare and Medicaid. In 2017, those politically volatile funds made up just 5% of the company's revenue.

Welltower has been steadily buying up quality properties in its target markets. In 2017 alone it spent $742 million to buy 26 new properties. As the company adds new properties to its portfolio, its revenue continues to grow. It collects rent and makes money on fees and services for its residents.

What's even better about Welltower is how relatively young its properties are. Just like people, older buildings require more upkeep. This is even more true in the medical industry, in which allowances need to be made for new regulations and state-of-the-art equipment. A portfolio of newer buildings means lower costs with fewer maintenance issues and remodeling expenses.

So I like the fact that Welltower's average building is just 19 years old—nearly half the age of the average health care REIT's buildings. And it has a few new projects in the works that show just how innovative this company is.

Consider its strategic partnership with Simon Property Group. Simon is best known as the owner-operator of shopping malls around the world. In 2017, Welltower announced it would add an outpatient medical facility to Simon's The Shops at Mission Viejo in California. So it will be nestled among shops and restaurants, as well as close to a nearby hospital. Can you think of a more convenient place for a doctor's office?

While Welltower continues to restructure itself to meet people's pressing medical needs, there is one thing it's been fairly consistent on—its dividend payouts. The company steadily increased its dividend every year from 2007 to 2017. That's a decade of higher payouts, even during the financial crisis in 2008–09. It doesn't get much better than that!

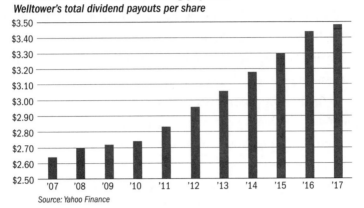

Welltower's decade of increasing payouts
Welltower's total dividend payouts per share

Source: Yahoo Finance

I think we have enough information to run this through our Three Pillars checklist!

Capital preservation: Welltower is one of the oldest health care REITs you can buy, with a history of adjusting its strategy to meet modern medical needs. Management has proven that it won't hesitate to sell assets if needed—and with a portfolio full of high-quality assets, it can expect top dollar from them. All these points should fill you with confidence.

Growth: People will always need to spend money to stay healthy, and Welltower has switched its business model to target the fastest-growing segment of the market. Its innovative partnerships and projects will keep it at the front of the pack, leading to more revenue while its younger buildings keep costs down. A lot to like here!

Yield: Take another look at the company's divided chart over the past decade. Ten full years of growth, even during one of the worst market periods in recent memory. If you had invested $5,000 in the company in 2007 and reinvested your dividends, you'd have been sitting on over $11,000 at the end of 2017. There's no reason not to expect the company to repeat that feat over the next decade.

This one is as close to a no-brainer as it gets. You can bet Washington politicians have noticed Welltower's history of increasing payouts . . . and now you can collect regular checks alongside them.

Action to take: Consider buying shares of Welltower (WELL).

Welltower has only traded under the symbol WELL since February 2018. Before that, it had the symbol HCN. That might affect some of the historical information you see on financial websites. The company's tax identification number is 34-1096634.

CHAPTER 15:

REGULAR CHECKS THANKS TO REGULAR CHECKUPS

Our final "Congressional Checks" opportunity is also a REIT that focuses on health care. It's called **Medical Properties Trust (MPW)**.

It's a lot newer than HCP and Welltower. Medical Properties Trust was founded in 2003 by hospital industry veterans to specialize exclusively on hospitals and related properties. And while its competitors have shifted their businesses toward senior living facilities, Medical Properties Trust has stuck to its guns.

The company owns 275 properties, all hospitals in one form or another. The bulk of them, 161 to be exact, are "general acute care hospitals"—the kind of places you think of when someone mentions the word "hospital." Another 97 are inpatient rehabilitation hospitals, where people recover from major surgeries and injuries. And the final 17 are long-term acute care hospitals. These are for patients who have complex medical needs and require long-term care.

Now, you probably see the problem here. In the last chapter, I told you that hospital admissions were on the decline. So Medical Properties Trust's hospital focus may seem like a bad thing. But the company's management has already taken that into consideration.

For one thing, it chooses its properties very carefully. The hospitals it buys are generally the only ones serving their communities. It also looks for hospitals where local doctors have offices. These are places patients go to for care even if they aren't taking up a hospital bed. Another thing management looks for are neighborhoods with higher-income demographics, so they have more paying patients.

Medical Properties Trust specializes in hospitals
MPW's total actual revenue by asset type

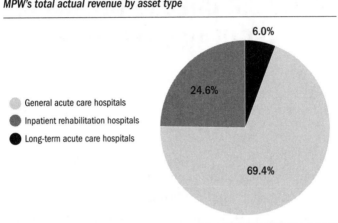

Source: Medical Properties Trust

Once a hospital is established, an entire infrastructure is built around it. Doctors' offices and physical therapy locations spring up next door. A whole network of services and vendors builds up around it. And once that infrastructure is in place, the real estate company owning the properties can enjoy the benefits of tenants who are extremely motivated to keep their existing locations.

The company also keeps a geographically diverse portfolio. While most of its properties are found in 29 U.S. states, it also owns facilities in the United Kingdom, Italy, Spain and Germany. Its most lucrative property represents just 3.7% of Medical Properties Trust's assets, meaning it could shut down entirely without ruining the company. And MPW works with 31 different medical groups, giving it a diverse client base.

It invests in hospitals in one of four ways.

First, it uses sale/leaseback transactions. This is where a hospital company raises cash by selling its building to Medical Properties, which in turn leases it back to the hospital company.

It's actually a brilliant setup for both parties. The building (and the land it sits on) is an asset that would otherwise just sit on a hospital's balance sheet. So selling it generates cash for the hospital. And leasing the building from Medical Properties turns the building into an operating expense—which a for-profit hospital can deduct against taxable revenues.

Then it signs a triple net lease, which means the tenant is responsible for taxes, insurance and operating expenses, which limits MPW's costs and uncertainty while allowing it to lock in a steady cash flow.

The second way Medical Properties grows is through new construction. The company's management is skilled at gaining tricky government approvals and then setting up the most competitive facilities in that local market. The company built a total of 19 facilities for Adeptus Health in 2016, which it then leased to Adeptus for a minimum of 15 years. And in December 2017 it started work on an 88-bed hospital in Idaho Falls, Idaho.

A third way is to invest in rehabbing and expanding existing hospitals. A prime example is in Houston, Texas, where the company rehabbed and expanded North Cypress Medical Center. Medical Properties funded the expansion and improvement while also doing a sale/leaseback. Now the hospital is as inviting to patients as a five-star hotel.

And finally, the company lends money to medical groups to buy hospitals. About 20% of the company's assets consist of these mortgage loans. As is the case with other REITs, they represent property that Medical Properties Trust could repossess if necessary.

Each of these business lines would provide a steady stream of cash if Medical Properties Trust did nothing else but collect its checks. But instead, the company continues to look for opportunities to build its collection of properties. It spent $95 million on acquisitions in 2017, which helped boost the company's assets by 33%. It also helped boost its revenues significantly.

In 2016, MPW raked in about $541 million. 2017's numbers blew that away, topping $704 million—a 30% increase. From that it extruded $289 million in income, a nice jump from 2016's $225 million income.

Medical Properties Trust's revenue and profits just continue to rise

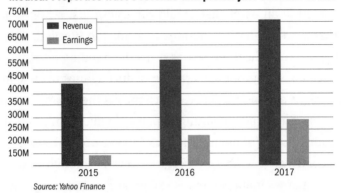

Source: Yahoo Finance

And despite having to fund all that growth, Medical Properties Trust hasn't been stingy with its dividend. The company has boosted its payouts every year since 2013. Again, that's exactly what we want to see when we invest our money in a company.

Medical Properties Trust's steady dividend boosts
MPW's total dividend per share

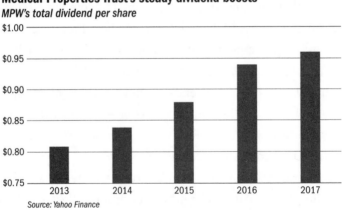

Source: Yahoo Finance

This one should pass the Three Pillars screening with flying colors.

Capital preservation: Medical Properties Trust has focused on developing great business relationships with hospitals, and there's no company that does it better. While overall hospital admissions are dropping, MPW's team has carefully selected its partners in great areas.

Growth: The company has a great collection of solid, high-revenue-producing hospital properties in high demand and limited supply in the market. Its revenue and earnings have taken off to match. And health care costs are expected to continue skyrocketing. It all points to Medical Properties Trust having a bright future.

Yield: Like Welltower, Medical Properties Trust has been on a dividend-boosting spree lately. But it's also kept enough money to expand its operations wisely, bringing in more revenue. It's a pretty virtuous cycle, and one I recommend becoming part of.

The bottom line is that Medical Properties Trust offers an alternative way to approach the booming health care market. Hospitals may not be as important as they once were, but they're also not in danger of dying out, either. And MPW will send you regular checks as long as people keep going for checkups.

Action to take: Consider buying shares of Medical Properties Trust (MPW).

Medical Properties Trust trades under the symbol MPW. Its tax identification number is 20-0191742.

BEGIN COLLECTING YOUR "CONGRESSIONAL CHECKS"

You've really got to hand it to the politicians. The Tax Cuts and Jobs Act of 2017 will likely prove to be one of the most beneficial pieces of legislation passed under President Trump. Our economy is set to thrive as employers boost salaries and employees keep more of that hard-earned money.

But passing the law also meant giving wealthy politicians one of the most blatant payoffs in recent memory. Senators and congressmen will see their tax bills plummet thanks to the REIT and FTE exclusions carved out by their addition of Section 199A to the U.S. tax code. They're lining up to receive some of the $1.7 trillion that's set to be paid out in 2018.

So I rushed this book into production to give you a chance to claim a portion of those payouts for yourself.

The companies I've shared could add thousands of dollars to your bank account every year. I know this for a fact, because readers of my newsletter *Lifetime Income Report* have written in to tell me about the payouts they've received.

There was Chris T., a retiree in Colorado. He bought 3,000 shares of Annaly Capital Management, the company I discussed in Chapter 8. Thanks to his purchase, he was poised to collect a check for $900 every quarter—and more after that, as Annaly raised its dividend.

There was also Justin F. He invested in the Blackstone Group, which I introduced in Chapter 6. His shares make him eligible to receive some of the $1.32 billion the company earns every year. When he wrote me, he was looking forward to receiving a $2,975 check.

Keep in mind I received these letters before the tax law passed. If Chris and Justin have held onto their shares, they'll be sending fewer dollars to the IRS this year than they have before!

I hope you enjoy similar success. In fact, I'd love to receive a letter from you telling me how much you've collected or stand to collect. Just shoot me an email at **AskZach@AgoraFinancial.com.**

Remember, earning this money couldn't be simpler. Open a brokerage account, use the symbols I've provided to find the stocks you want to buy and then purchase some shares. Within three months, your first checks will arrive—and will, hopefully, keep growing from there.

Also remember to monitor your positions carefully. Every company I've named in this book is a stock that is traded between investors. Each has the ability to rise and fall in price. So there is a risk of loss, especially if the general stock market gets in trouble.

And finally, while I believe the Tax Cuts and Jobs Act of 2017 will help you keep more of the cash you earn from these companies, everyone's tax situation is different. Be sure to check with a tax adviser to make sure "Congressional Checks" will benefit you as much as they benefit the politicians who voted for the law.

With that, it's now all up to you. Best of luck!